Last Summer

Lily Grace

Lily Grace

Note from the author

Hi!! Thank you for picking this book up and deciding to read it, oh my god, thank you.

If you relate to Cecelia, please get help. ♡

Seriously though, if you struggle with intrusive thoughts, suicidal ideation, or anxiety, there are a lot of resources out there to help you. I love you, please get help.

Trigger warnings

Anxiety, depression, eating disorders, intrusive thoughts, body dysphoria, body dysmorphia, suicidal ideation, and panic attacks.

This book is for you, the reader. I love

you more than words can describe, and I want

to give you a hug and chocolate. I can't do that

for all of you, so I'm giving you a book.

Chapter One

This summer needs to be a summer like no other. It's my last one before I go to university, the last one before I'm a real adult. It doesn't feel real. Nothing feels real anymore.

Although, a summer like no other might be hard to accomplish since I'm not a summer person. I'm more of an autumn/winter person. I look my best in a cozy sweater, my chestnut hair pulled back behind a headband. Blistering sun, too-short shorts, and sunburn lines aren't my thing. I love having time off from school, but this season takes so much energy. I wish it was always winter or autumn.

But no matter what I think, summer comes, so I've taught myself to like it. I've learned to appreciate the way my freckles multiply, spreading their way across my pale nose and cheeks. I've found a way to love the free time to hang out with my friends, make bucket lists, and swim. I've figured out how to enjoy sticky popsicles and warm soda.

This being said, the first day of summer is one of the best days of the year. After Christmas, of course. And every day leading up to Christmas. I love Christmas.

Okay, after Christmas. The first day of summer is unmatched. It's got a certain vibe to it that no other day can replicate. You only get twelve first days of summer in your life, at least the kind that count. So far, I've wasted three first days wallowing in self-pity. Middle school is the shittiest place in the world. It doesn't matter anymore. Elementary school barely counts; it's a time for summer camps and family vacations.

But high school. My first days of summer in high school have been the best days of my life. By this point, I've found people that make it worth it to be alive in the summer. My gang, if you will. We've spent every first day of summer for the past four years together, and that tradition will not stop today.

"Who brought chips?" Roxanne tosses her dark hair aside to rifle through our bags.

"I didn't, I figured you would." I shrug. Chips are an essential part of summer. Are you even having fun if you're not eating chips?

"I don't bring the chips, I just eat them! Cecelia, in seventeen years of friendship, I'd expect you to know this by now," she groans, falling backwards on my bed dramatically. "Do you have any?" she asks Jessie, who shakes their head of floppy blonde hair.

"What are you gonna do, bro?" Otto smirks, sunlight reflecting off his hollow copper cheeks and ebony hair. "Are you gonna survive?"

"No, I don't think so. We need to go buy some." She leaps up from the beanbag she's sitting on and reaches out her hand to Jessie.

"Seriously?" I snort. "We're going to leave my nice air-conditioned house, go outside where it's a hundred degrees, basically die, just to get chips?"

"Are chips really worth all that?" Otto says, raising an eyebrow.

"Is that even a question? Come on, let's go. It's summer! We can go swimming or something after." She grabs Jessie's hand and pulls them up. I always forget how crazy their height difference is until I see them side by side, Jessie's lanky body looming over Roxanne's measly five feet and two inches.

At the mention of swimsuits, Otto and Jessie share a look of discomfort.

"Maybe we can get popsicles at the store," I suggest, standing up beside Roxie. Otto sighs, but he rises to his feet using my shoulder as a crutch. I force all three of them to put sunscreen on, not accepting any of their protests. No one is dying of skin cancer on my watch.

The heat hits us like a ton of bricks. My ponytail swishes back and forth over my shoulders and sticks to the sweat on my neck. **Rip it out.** Haha, no thanks. I tie it up into a messy bun to hopefully end the snaky stream of intrusive thoughts sliding into my brain.

Muriel's Corner Store is literally three blocks from my house, but it's the longest three blocks of my life. I have been going to Muriel's since I could walk. You can literally buy anything there. It's like my holy grail in the summertime.

Inside, Roxanne picks out a family-sized bag of salt and vinegar chips plus a bag of Cheezies. I grab three popsicles from the cooler and turn to look at Otto.

"Do ya want one?" I ask. He shakes his head and takes an iced tea out of the fridge.

"Nah, I'll just have this instead."

The gang keeps telling me that I should buy our things to work on my 'social anxiety' because, apparently, it's 'exposure therapy'. I think I can do this because Muriel is working at the till. Muriel is always working at the till. She's so nice and I know she'd never judge me. I place the snacks on the counter and take out my wallet.

"Hey there, Cecelia." Muriel smiles a nice old lady smile. "How's it been, doll?"

"Pretty good. I'm really glad it's summer."

"That's nice to hear you're doing better." She puts the items in a bag and passes them back to me. I didn't think my anxiety was improving that much, but it's nice to hear. I wave goodbye and head back outside. My friends are sitting on the curb playing the license plate game.

"7-7!" I shout, punching all three of them.

"Owwww!" Otto yells.

"That doesn't count, I saw it first." Roxanne takes the bag from me and pulls out the chips, hugging them tightly to her chest before opening the bag up. She hands us each our popsicles and gives Otto his iced tea.

The cherry-red popsicle almost makes up for the scalding heat of the air, but the pavement still burns my thighs below my skirt.

"Okay fine, we got chips, but can we go to the lake now?" I slump against the sidewalk like I'm melting from the sun. "I'm literally dying."

The town we live in is named after the lake — Lake Oublie.

"I guess so... but our bathing suits are at our houses," Jessie says slowly. All of our houses are within three feet of each other, but I know that that's not why they don't want to wear one. It's difficult for them to find the line between an androgynous swimsuit and one that doesn't raise too much suspicion from family friends. I can never decide if I love or hate how tiny our town is. Knowing everyone is cool, but it means everyone knows you. That's less cool. Otto also doesn't want to wear his swim trunks but for completely unrelated reasons.

"Let's just go in our clothes?" I offer.

"Ugh, but I'm wearing jean shorts!" Roxanne complains. **She hates you.** God, why does my brain do that? That was so unnecessary.

"I think you'll survive," Jessie snorts, swinging their arm around her shoulders and staring lovingly into her eyes.

I turn away from Roxie and Jessie's sappy romance and break out into a run towards the beach, taking the shortcut through the woods. The faster I go, the sooner I'll cool down, right?

Otto catches up to me in no time, swinging his arm around my shoulders when he does. In the woods, the trees fan out like a canopy, hiding us from the blazing sun.

"Did you know that when Roxie and I were little, we'd call this the fairy forest?" I say, grinning at the memory.

He raises an eyebrow at me and stifles a giggle.

"What?! From some angles, the ferns look like fairy wings." I huff.

"Oh yeah, I guess that makes – RACE YOU!" He shouts, catching me off guard.

"HEY!"

Otto beats me to the beach. By the time I get there, he's lying down on the gray sand, his chest rising and falling in rhythm with the waves. I go straight into the water, soaking my corduroy skirt on the way in. Otto sits up, takes his hoodie off, and joins me in the lake. Even though I know why he gets so cold, it's still baffling that he can wear a hoodie in this weather. He shivers a bit from the cool water, but I find it delightfully soothing.

Roxanne and Jessie emerge from the trees visibly sweating. They both collapse into the waves, splashing me as they do. I take a shaky breath watching kids play around us without a care in the world, something I haven't been able to do in years. **You don't deserve to.**

"You guys, we should totally do a chicken fight!" Roxanne exclaims, breaking my brain from the dangerous spiral it was starting. Without letting anyone reply, she pushes on my shoulders, urging me to let her on. I reluctantly do so, nearly toppling over when she climbs on.

Otto pulls himself onto Jessie's shoulders and furrows his brows.

"Let's do this thing!" They charge towards us and try to knock Roxanne over. She grabs hold of Otto's shoulders and tries to push him sideways, making them both Jessie and Otto go toppling down to the water. Roxanne and I cheer wildly, making people of all ages stare at us with raised eyebrows. **They think you're really weird.** The air whooshes out of my lungs at the thought, but when I look at Otto and Jessie tumbling in the waves, I let out a little laugh. It doesn't matter if people think we're weird, we're having fun. Almost, *almost*, without a care in the world.

Chapter Two

Wet sand squishes under my palms as I'm thrown to the ground. Again. We switched partners after Roxanne and I lost, so now I'm with Otto.

"I demand a rematch!" he shouts.

"Dude, we've already done five," Roxanne groans. "We don't need to do another."

The hotter the day gets, the more people spill onto the shore. Kids squeal around us, splashing water in our direction. My throat starts to close up as I imagine the germs pooling around us. The crowds are starting to close in on me. Even though my head is above water, I feel like I'm drowning.

"I have to go," I whisper, a panicked tone to my voice. The quiet pitch is all I can muster through my closed throat.

Roxanne nods and puts her arm around my shoulder, leading me through the mob. The others follow behind us.

I collapse onto my couch the second we arrive at my house.

"You're sure that your parents are okay with this?" Otto takes a seat beside me.

"You guys have been coming over for four years, I think they're fine with y'all sleeping over by now." My family doesn't even give it a second thought at this point. The first time everyone slept over, my parents were a little suspicious of Otto and Jessie. I had to tell them that Jessie and Roxie were dating for them to trust Jessie. It was a bit harder for me to convince them that Otto and I weren't an item. It was only when I came out to them as asexual that they finally understood that my feelings for him are platonic. He also brought his ex-girlfriend around a couple of times, so that helped.

Every single time we have a sleepover, we argue for ages about what movie to watch. I'm a big rom-com fan, Roxanne loves horror, Jessie's into tear-jerker dramas, and Otto likes anything with well-directed action scenes. We've agreed on a sort of rotation between the genres. Tonight is a horror night.

Roxanne selects a psychological thriller, ignoring Jessie and my's complaints.

"This looks terrifying!" I gasp as she plays the trailer.

"That's the point." She rolls her eyes "Y'all will be fine," she assures us. "Did you bring Floppy?"

Jessie reaches into their backpack and pulls out the worn beige rabbit I know so well. I smile, knowing Floppy's ears have dried our tears, his paws have helped us hide our eyes from scary scenes, and he's been stress-cuddled until his stuffing has deflated.

Roxanne won him at a carnival in ninth grade and he's been our mascot ever since. This bunny knows more about me than my parents do.

I reach over and snatch Floppy from Jessie's grasp as Roxanne presses play on the movie. Dramatic cello starts playing while the camera zooms in on a terrified girl in a wedding dress. I squeeze Floppy tight and bury my face in his fur.

"Come on Cecelia, it's not even that scary yet!" Roxanne yells, throwing a pillow at my head. "Also what are we gonna have for dinner?"

"Oh yeah! I was gonna order pizza but I forgot." I take out my phone and dial the number of our local pizza joint.

"Anyone wanna do the talking for me?" I request. They all shake their heads.

"You gotta do it, dude." Otto squeezes my shoulder in reassurance. I press pause on the movie and click the call button, trying to ignore the rising feeling of dread in my stomach. A young man with an Italian accent answers.

"Hi um... can – can I get a large cheese pizza and a small salad please?" **You sound ridiculous.** My voice is caught in my throat and sounds a lot squeakier than normal. The dude on the other end doesn't seem to notice and says the food will be here in twenty minutes.

I resume the movie but continue to talk over it so I won't get scared. "Okay, until that arrives, list everyone you've ever liked. Go!" I point at Jessie.

"Uh I forget everyone, but Roxanne obviously and like two girls from summer camp but that's pretty much it," they say, nodding at Otto to go next.

"Um... some people from middle school, and...um...Gail..."

We all groan out of disgust at the mention of Otto's ex's name. I fake a gag as Roxanne boos. We hate Gail more than words can describe. She was awful. Just terrible.

"And Roxie, haha."

17

Roxanne flips her hair dramatically. "What can I say? I'm just amazing. Everyone is in love with me."

I roll my eyes and hit her in the head with the pillow she threw at me. "Whatever. It's your turn."

"Hmmm.... Jessie and..." She goes on to list the 'queen bee' of sixth grade and every member from her girl band in middle school. She dated one of the members of that short-lived band for a brief time. Roxanne's got a shot with literally anyone she wishes. I find it hilarious that both Jessie and Otto — who are cousins — and Otto's little brother, all liked her. She's gone through the whole family tree.

"Okay, can we keep watching the movie now?" she requests, turning towards the TV. The red light from the screen reflects onto her side profile, highlighting every one of her perfect features.

Sometimes I wish I was Roxie. Not for everything, but for lots of things.

I wish I was as pretty as her. Her deep-set honey-colored eyes stand out against her tawny face. She always glows, inside and out. **You'll never be as pretty as her.**

I wish I was as confident as her. She doesn't let people tell her that her hooked nose or size fourteen body makes her any less attractive. She holds herself with a confidence that makes her ten times hotter than any skinny, white, rhinoplastied model. **You'll never be as confident as her.**

I wish I was as mentally stable as her. She's the only one in our group that has never needed to see a psychiatrist. **You'll never be as stable as her.** She definitely doesn't have that voice in her head. Or, if she does, she definitely never listens to it.

Dinner arrives, tearing the group out of the scary movie and tearing me out of my spiralling thoughts. I volunteer to go get it, passing my mom on the way.

"You ordered pizza?" she queries, her eyebrows raised in surprise.

"Yeah, of course." I stare at her, puzzled. We get pizza all the time, why would that be weird? I open the door and pay the guy with a twenty-dollar bill.

"Keep the change," I mumble, trying not to make eye contact when I realize he's my ninth-grade teacher's son. **He probably knows how crazy you were in ninth grade.**

I bring the food back downstairs, setting the pizza on the coffee table and the salad in front of Otto. His middle school friends would've called him a pussy or something for being scared of the calories in the pizza. I just pat him on the back.

"It's gonna be okay. You'll be able to eat it one day, I promise," I whisper.

"Thanks." He smiles slightly before stabbing his fork into the salad. Roxanne presses play on the movie and we resume our shrieks of fear.

Although we're all laughing and joking around, I know that there's one thing that's weighing heavily on all of our minds. Something we're all thinking about that none of us have the balls to talk about.

Next year.

College.

We're all going to different places. We're all leaving this province. Jessie is going to Oxford for English Literature. Roxanne is taking a gap year and traveling through Europe. Otto got into art school in California. I'm going into creative writing in Quebec. We'll all have different roommates and different time zones. Roxie will meet thousands of new and interesting people around the world. We'll only see each other on holidays, if that.

What does that mean for us?

Chapter Three

Ninth Grade, January

Freshman year hasn't been a very good year for me so far. Middle school sucked ass; I couldn't make a friend to save my life. The only person at this high school I know is Roxanne, my family friend who is ten times cooler than I'll ever be. **She only talks to you because she pities you.**

> *My days are a boring repetitive cycle.*
>
> *Wake up.*
>
> *Dread going to school.*
>
> *Cry.*
>
> *Walk to school with Roxanne.*
>
> *Classes.*
>
> *Wallow in self-hatred.*
>
> *Wish I could make a friend for once.*

Eat lunch in Ms. Wilson's classroom alone.

Panic attack.

Read.

Walk home with Roxanne.

Homework.

Cry.

Try to sleep.

Repeat.

I hate it. I wish I was someone else. Anyone else.

The panic attacks are becoming too much to handle. Schoolwork piles up and the thought of my future terrifies me. My emotions range from mediocre to wanting to die, and I hate myself constantly. Only a few things relax me. I love reading romance novels and watching the occasional cheesy hospital soap opera. Any extra time I have, I spend watching self-care videos on the internet. I write lists and plan glow–ups I'll never commit to. I pretend I'm someone else.

*Sometimes, Roxanne will come over to hang out with me. **Her parents make her.** She'll sit with me and we'll watch movies. She'll tell me all the drama in her friend group because she knows I won't tell anyone. I have no one to tell anyway.*

Today, her whole family is over at my house. Our parents are in the living room drinking cocktails and gossiping, while Roxie and I are in my room, drinking sugary soda and gossiping. Well, she's gossiping. I'm listening.

"Okay, well, I think I might like someone new." She grins, staring off into space.

*I gasp. "Who is it?!" I think I might be living vicariously through Roxie sometimes, pretending I'm someone who can giggle with friends about crushes and not be caught up with intrusive thoughts and impending doom. **As if.***

"You know Jessie Diaz? They're in the GSA. Blonde hair, light academia...?"

"Oh yeah, I know them! I always love their sweaters!" Jessie Diaz is known for their aesthetic. They look like they stepped right out of a mood board full of sweater vests, corduroy pants, and vanilla lattes. Everything they wear is shades of brown and cream, even the minimalist makeup they do.

"Yeah, um... I'm thinking of asking them out." She smiles softly to herself.

"Really?" The first image that comes to mind isn't of Jessie. It's of their cousin, Otto. He's in my homeroom and I've always found him incredibly cool. He is friends with a big group of dickheads, but he seems different. He's an amazing artist and he's always writing in a journal. I'm so envious of the way he acts. I wish more than anything that I could be him. I wish I could be

the artsy guy in a giant friend group. It's very difficult when you want to be that, yet you're the anxious girl with no friends. Maybe Roxanne dating Jessie will be an opportunity for Otto and I to actually become friends. It sounds ridiculous, I know, but I can't help but feel a little bit of hope at the prospect of it.

"That's incredible. You totally should," I encourage her.

"Are you just saying that cuz you wanna be friends with Otto?" She rolls her eyes. Roxie is the only person I've told about anything like that. She's the only person I can tell. She might not be able to relate, but at least she isn't mean or judgy about it. She just thinks the way I act about it is funny. Which I guess it kinda is.

"A little bit, but I also think you'd be good together." I feel like they'd balance each other out well—Jessie's quiet calmness paired with Roxanne's outgoing energy.

"You know, you could ask Otto out if you wanted," she lets me know.

"Ew no, I don't like him that way."

"Okay, just putting that out there." She shrugs.

I haven't told anyone I'm asexual yet. I figure I'll wait a while, just until I'm sure. I used to wonder if I just hadn't met the right person yet, but now I'm almost certain that I'm aroace. When I do tell someone, it'll be Roxanne. I just have to find the right time to come out. I have never had a romantic crush ever in my life. The difference between a romantic crush and a platonic crush is something I don't know how to explain. A platonic crush is just desperately wanting to be friends with someone and finding them incredibly intriguing. I get at least one per year, none of whom I've actually befriended. **Of course you haven't.**

"*I just really want to be his friend,*" *I tell her. She tilts her head to look at me, which leads me to believe I'm the only person in the world who feels this way about people. Like we would be incredibly close if I only had the guts to talk to him.* **You never will.** *Yeah, thanks, I know.*

Images fill my brain of Roxanne telling her friends, them laughing, spreading rumors, everyone thinking I'm in love with him, needing to come out, needing to explain it, no one believing me.

They wouldn't care. They wouldn't care. No one cares.

That is the message I have to tell myself when the crazy social anxiety starts firing up. Try to convince myself that no one cares about me. It's not great for the general anxiety that convinces me I'm going to get murdered on a back road and not have my body found for weeks, but it occasionally works for the 'everyone is judging me' stuff. My therapist might have some

25

opinions about that coping strategy, but it's fine. **She doesn't care that much.**

No one cares.

"Dude, where did you go?" Roxanne waves a hand in front of my face, bringing me back to the real world. I've found myself zoning out a lot lately, too caught up in my brain spiraling to stay on Earth.

"I'm here." I shake my head to stop it from happening again. *"Wanna watch a movie?"*

"Always," she replies.

"What movie do you want to watch?"

"Can it be a horror movie?"

Chapter Four

The sun wakes me up the next morning. It still doesn't feel real that it's summer. Sunbeams glow like highlighter on everyone's faces. Jessie and Roxanne are soundly asleep in my bed, Roxie's arms wrapped around Jessie's torso. Otto is sprawled out on the floor where we've haphazardly placed spare mattresses and couch cushions to create two makeshift beds for him and I.

I tend to be the first to wake up out of the four of us. I wake up early during the school year, so my internal clock is set to six a.m. I stretch my arms above my head and take my book off my bedside table.

The story I'm currently invested in is a romance. Despite not having a desire for one of my own, I eat up novels about love and its complications. I love the predictability and safety of a good love story. In this one, two girls that hate each

27

other pretend to date to make their exes jealous. Spoiler alert: they fall in love. Like I said, predictable.

You know what isn't predictable? Real life. That is why I always prefer to live life through paper and pen. I read stories and I write them, just to pretend that I don't have to deal with waking up another day. I think a lot of people that struggle with mental illness do something similar. Jessie is like me, spending days at their computer crafting intricate worlds.

Otto is different from us. He doesn't live his life through literature. He lives it through art. His portraits and stills depict things he's never been able to say out loud. When you look at something he's made, you feel as though you are in his head, seeing his thoughts play out in front of you. It really is incredible. I've never seen anything quite like it.

Roxanne isn't like the rest of us. She doesn't need to live her life vicariously through something else. She lives it for herself. She doesn't use words or art to make a difference, she does it purely through her own presence. Real life is good enough for her. Real life is kind enough to her.

Jessie is the next to wake up. They sit up in bed, their sun-coloured hair a total mess. We tend to be on a similar schedule, early birds as opposed to night owls like the other two.

"Wanna help me make breakfast?" I whisper, trying not to wake up our unconscious buddies.

"Yeah, sure." They stand up and step over the lump under the blankets that is Otto. Our socks pitter-patter against the floorboards as we decide what to make.

"Waffles?" they suggest.

"Too much effort." I sigh.

"French toast?"

"Not enough effort."

"I don't know man! You choose."

"What about pancakes?" Pancakes are the perfect breakfast food. They taste good with literally any toppings.

"Yeah, that works."

They start to get the ingredients together as I attempt to pull out the skillet without making too much noise. It's difficult, considering the pan is at the very bottom of the drawer. I eventually manage to get it out, but it's a struggle.

At this point, Jessie and I have memorized every recipe in our rotation. We cycle through pancakes, waffles, french toast, crepes, and the occasional scones if we're feeling fancy. The cooking of the pancakes is like a perfectly rehearsed ballet, every step and move anticipated and steady. I hand them the flour as they reach a measuring cup in. They stir the dry

29

ingredients as I split the shells of two eggs. They set the table as I pour the batter. We listen to music through shared earbuds and dance around the kitchen to early 2000s hits.

Otto and Roxanne stumble down the stairs, looking like they've been sleeping for hundreds of years. Otto's eyebags look hollow and deep purple in the morning light. Sometimes I forget that he wears concealer during the day. I forget about the pain and insomnia stored under his eyes. He always tries to mask it with a smile and with laughing and boob jokes. Oftentimes, we forget. Otto never gets to forget.

The two of them sit down at the table as Jessie and I place pancakes on their plates. Jessie sits down at one head of the table and I sit down at the other, spraying whipped cream from an aerosol can on my stack of pancakes. Roxanne covers her pile in chocolate syrup, placing a single strawberry on top.

"So, I was thinking last night," she starts, stealing the whipped cream from in front of me.

"That's new." Otto snorts. Roxie throws a strawberry at his head, which he promptly catches in mid-air.

"Annnyways. This is our last summer together." A collective groan resounds around the room. "It needs to be incredible. We need to do things we've never imagined. We need.... a bucket list," she announces, throwing her hands in the air.

Otto and I burst out laughing. "How old are we?" I ask. "Nine?"

"No. We're seventeen. And in two months, we'll never hang out again. Sure we'll text and everything, but it'll never be the same. We'll never be teenagers again. So this summer needs to be the best summer ever. We need to have reasons to remember it." Roxanne stares at us individually. The three of us look at each other. We all have reasons to remember our friendships. We have the fact that we're not dead to prove they existed.

"Okaaay. What do you propose we add to this list?" I ask.

"I mean... I have a bunch of ideas. Skinny dipping, for one." She smirks. I choke on my mango juice and Otto makes a strange guffawing sound. Jessie just raises their eyebrows at Roxanne. "I wrote a whole list last night when y'all fell asleep. Hold on, I'll go get it."

"She's insane." I shake my head.

"Yeah." Jessie smiles, a dreamy look in their eyes. "I'm gonna marry her someday."

31

Otto chuckles and looks down at his pancakes, his smile fading when he sees the untouched mound. I kick his leg lightly so he looks up at me. I smile and nod slightly. It's going to be okay.

Roxanne comes back downstairs, phone in hand. She opens her notes app and starts to read out loud.

"Number one! Go to a carnival."

"I mean, that's pretty normal." I shrug.

"It gets worse," she warns. "Number two, reinvent ourselves for university."

"Is that necessary?" Jessie asks.

"Absolutely." Otto and I say simultaneously. We both need somewhat of a wardrobe update.

"Number three, as I've previously said, go skinny dipping. Four, go cliff jumping."

A shiver of anxiety runs through my spine at the idea of that one.

"Five, attend a wedding. Six, attend a funeral."

"Where are we gonna find either of those?" I wonder.

"I don't know, somewhere." She shrugs. "Seven, sneak in somewhere. Eight, get tattoos."

"Are you kidding me?!" Jessie gasps. They've always been sort of the parent-friend. Always bringing snacks and never encouraging 'bad behavior'. Hilarious that they're dating Roxanne, the ultimate bad-influence friend.

"Yes! We have to get tattoos to remind us of The Best Summer Ever!" Roxanne cheers.

"We'll discuss it." I roll my eyes. "What's next?"

"Nine, come out to my parents," Jessie says, almost quiet enough to be a whisper. There's a moment of silence before Roxanne nods and types it into her notes.

"Ten, we have to egg Gail's house," she says decisively. Otto's mouth drops open at the mention of his shitty ex. I cheer loudly and Jessie offers Roxanne a high-five for thinking of the idea.

"I don't think that's–" Otto starts.

"Nope, it's necessary. Eleven, go shopping for dorm supplies and decorate our rooms together."

A soft smile plays on my lips as I imagine that scene. "It sounds perfect."

Chapter Five

"So, where do we start?" Otto asks, cutting his pancakes into little squares.

"Well, I was thinking that we could go shopping today. For the reinventing part," Roxanne says.

"We have to make mood boards for inspiration though." Jessie pulls out their phone and texts their board to the group chat. It looks essentially like what they currently wear, but a bit more dignified with a bit more, queer per se. Lots of sweater vests, androgynous skirts, and plaid pants. Many hats.

I think Jessie is really looking forward to escaping Lake Oublie and going to university so they can finally express themselves how they've always wanted.

A text chimes on our phones from Roxanne. Apparently, she also had a mood board of clothes completely ready for this moment. Her board consists of lots of jean skirts, band tees, and leather jackets. In a cool way, not the poseur way. She can't wear a lot of these in Lake Oublie — the catholic old women would throw a fit at some of the album covers. She's got a couple of graphic tees right now, but they're all pretty toned down. She has one that I am absolutely obsessed with; coffee coloured and oversized with a vintage map of Manhattan on it. I steal it every chance I get. Although we all have different styles of clothing, we somehow share clothes all the time.

"Did everyone get the memo that we were supposed to make one of these?" Otto wonders, zooming in on Roxie's photos.

"I only really have a mental one," I tell him.

"Don't worry, we'll help y'all pick out clothes when we get to the mall," Roxanne assures us. Jessie nods along. Otto and I raise our eyebrows at each other, unsure. Neither of their aesthetics really suit us. He's a lot more of a baggy jean/casual vibe and I tend to gravitate toward giant sweaters and plaid skirts. It makes it incredibly difficult to find outfits for summer, let me tell you.

Once we're finished eating breakfast, we head upstairs to get ready. It takes Otto three seconds to get ready because he wears the same baggy jeans and hoodie every day. The only makeup he uses is the concealer under his eyes, and he blends it with his fingers in approximately 0.5 seconds.

Roxanne does the opposite of that. She takes five minutes to choose an outfit from her drawer of clothes that she keeps at my house. The famous Manhattan tee-shirt, jean skirt, and a chunky belt.

Jessie and I start by doing skincare together, making ourselves feel put together and mentally stable. I apply mascara on my eyelashes and spread blush all over my cheeks and nose. Jessie slides brown eyeliner over their waterline, ending it in a little wing at the end. They use a little gold highlighter on their cheeks, nose, and in their inner corners. We hand each other brushes and wands in an unspoken rhythm. Roxanne enters the bathroom, pouring her supplies all over the sink counter, so we go back into my room to get dressed.

Jessie picks a simple outfit of black jean shorts and a button-up shirt.

I stand in front of my wardrobe, unable to make a decision. Otto reaches in and pulls out short overalls and a t-shirt. He hands them to me wordlessly. That's good enough. I put my hair in two braids hanging down my back, curtain bangs swooping over my face. My signature hairstyle.

Fifteen minutes later, Roxanne has finished her makeup. We're ready to go.

The mall is a good twenty-minute walk from our town. Usually, I'd drive, but Jessie keeps insisting that we should be exercising throughout the summer. So here we are, walking through all the depressing empty suburbs for what feels like years until we finally reach the gigantic mall. This mall is the most populated place within a hundred-kilometer radius.

And today, the second day of summer, it is full of sweaty hormonal teenagers with nothing else going on in their lives. Greasy fast food and overpriced department stores line the walls. Too white paint and nonsensical chatter fill my senses, no matter how hard I try to block it all out.

Usually, Roxanne will see a bunch of people she knows and talk to each and every single one of them. Jessie will pepper in small talk while Otto and I shift awkwardly in the background. For some reason, that doesn't happen today.

Everyone knows Roxie because she plays bass in the Jazz Band. It makes her sound like a nerd, but people that are in bands are admired at our school. It's somewhat like football in cliche high school movies set in the States. Apparently, where American kids admire football and cheer, Canadian kids admire bands and hockey. There's a reason Canada is portrayed so strangely in the media. It's because it is strange.

Roxanne sees a couple of people she knows, but they either wave or ignore us completely. She doesn't seem bothered by it, and I don't want to bring it up, because the best part of school is not needing to talk to kids from school.

Jessie steers us towards a department store bigger than my house, their second favorite place to buy clothes, after thrift stores.

Department stores stress me out. They're so big, yet somehow so crowded at the same time. My anxiety cannot handle it. I feel like I can hear every conversation on full volume. **Too loud. TOO LOUD. TOO LOUD!**

My hand reaches out to grab Otto's arm, the familiar feeling of his hoodie serving as a temporary comfort. He turns to look at me, his eyebrows raised in shock.

"You okay?" he asks. I'm pretty sure my panicked face is giving away the fact that I'm definitely not. As if on instinct, he takes my noise-canceling earbuds out of my bag and hands them to me. He takes my phone and starts to play my 'calm down' playlist. It's a lot of country music.

Unpopular opinion; country music is incredible. Sure, every song sounds the same and yeah, many of them are written by sexist homophobes. I can't count the number of songs that are guys talking about how their woman is perfect for them and talking about her like she's his property. All of that aside, the majority of country songs are bangers. Maybe that's just my opinion. Granted, I was raised in redneck Canada, but I'd like to think that country music isn't just a redneck thing. Despite the repetitive lyrics, I believe that all country songs have an important message. Almost every song is about enjoying the little things in life, like trucks and beer and good friends. Country music is beautiful in its own unique way.

That's why my entire 'calm down' playlist is made up of country music. My brain will stop thinking about whatever is scaring me and instead think about the messages behind the song and make up little stories about them. Everyone thinks it's weird that country music calms me, and I guess it is. I can't really explain how it feels. You just have to know.

The lyrics loop in my head and drown out the other sounds. The people sounds. Otto looks me in the eye and gives me a questioning look. I nod my head, only shaking slightly as I do. I back myself against a wall and stand there for a second, feeling the cold on my exposed shoulders and my feet on the ground. I close my eyes and take myself to my happy place.

I am no longer in the terrifying department store. I'm in a secret place in my mind. The place I can't describe to anyone because they wouldn't understand. I'm on a swing under a tree. My hands don't blister when they're wrapped around the ropes and my thighs don't stick to the sanded down driftwood. Sweet peaches hang around my head, their branches creating a perfect oasis of shade. My body sways back and forth. Back and forth. I'm weightless. Flying. My bare feet brush against the tips of wildflowers growing in the grass.

I count the things I can see. The things I can feel. The things I can–

"Yo, Cecelia, you good?" Roxanne's voice pulls me out of the peach tree. Out of the meadow. It's okay. I have my happy people here. I don't need my happy place.

"Yeah, I'm okay."

Roxanne is holding a handful of clothes. Jessie is standing beside her, an equal amount of items in their arms.

"We got you some stuff to try on," Jessie tells me, putting their pile in my arms.

"Oh wow okay." I chuckle.

Otto emerges from the clothing racks holding a green bandana. "I wanted to contribute somehow." He wraps the bandana around the top of my head and ties it below my braids. "Perfect."

***

"Okay, Cece. How do you want to be perceived in university?" Roxanne asks, sitting on the 'boyfriend couch' outside of the changing room. We've all been watching each other try on clothes and hyping each other up. I'm the only one that hasn't gone yet.

Roxanne had strutted out of the changing room in skintight band tees and tiny skirts. She'd shown us what they looked like from every angle and grinned at herself in the mirror, admiring how the crimson of her shirt complimented her dark hair. She's got a huge pile of stuff to buy. Clothes shopping is always easier for her than it is for the rest of us.

Jessie tried on clothes they'd never be able to wear around here, gender-affirming stuff that their old-fashioned catholic grandparents would disown them for. I could see the fear in their eyes when they stepped out from behind the curtain, but the euphoria when they looked in the mirror. I'm

41

so excited for them to be able to wear whatever they want in university.

Otto struggled the most. He tried on a couple of 'wife beater' style tank tops, but when he stepped out of the changeroom, he couldn't even look at himself in the mirror. We told him that he looked incredible, which he did, but he didn't listen. We've convinced him to buy one, the baggiest one. Baby steps.

Now I guess it's my turn.

"Cecelia! How do you wanna be perceived?" Roxanne repeats.

"Um, I don't know. Happy and mentally stable?" I shrug.

"But then how will they know you're cool?" Otto grins.

"Fine. Confident? Nice? I don't know."

"Confidence is easy," Roxanne says. "It's all fake."

"No way. Do not say 'fake it 'till you make it'. That's all bullshit." I sigh.

"Well... what makes you feel confident?" she asks.

I think over my wardrobe, trying to remember what makes me feel the least self-conscious. "Sweaters, maybe? They make me happy."

"Okay great. Buy sweaters!" She flops back on the couch like she's solved all my problems.

"I already have a lot of sweaters!"

Jessie speaks up from behind the couch. "What's something you wish you had the confidence to wear?"

"I don't know."

"Yes, you do."

"I guess... I'd like to be able to wear shorter shirts? There are so many good outfits with small shirts, like baby tees? I've never had the confidence to wear something like that."

You'd look awful in something like that. Everyone will laugh.

"Now you will!" Roxanne exclaims. "That's perfect! Go find one you like."

"....I don't know about that."

You will look ridiculous.

"Yes. Go find one. Or more, if you'd like."

"...Okay."

The aisles are filled with little shirts, the kind I was imagining, but I can't get myself to pick them up. That is, until I spot a deep green one with a lyric from one of my favorite singers. I know it'll be tight and short, but I love it too much to care.

43

As I'm returning to the changing room, I pass by a collection of crochet tops. I've never worn a crochet top before—they scare me too much. There's a really beautiful one, a lavender-coloured tank that criss-crosses in the back. I barely ever wear tank tops, my eczema shows too much. Before I can overthink it, I take it off the shelf and bring it with me.

"What did you get, what did you get?!" Roxanne urges the second I get back, pulling the shirts out of my hands. "These are so cute I love them! Try them on right now." She pushes me into a changeroom and shuts the curtain.

I hate changerooms. Especially the ones with no mirrors, the kind where you have to step out and look at yourself in front of everyone. **Everyone will judge you.** It's terrifying.

I take as much time as possible to change into the green shirt, dreading the big reveal. I haven't worn anything this tight since I was seven. I'm not sure I can do this.

Breathe.

I open the curtain and step out, bracing myself for what I'll look like. When I glance at myself in the mirror, disgust fills my stomach. **You look awful. Why did you think you could pull this off?**

"Cecelia..." Jessie starts, but I cut them off before they can finish.

"Yeah, I know. I look awful. I'm sorry, I'll change back into my normal outfit–"

"NO!" Roxanne shouts. "YOU LOOK INCREDIBLE!!! How have you not been wearing clothes like this all the time?! It totally suits you! Oh my god! Go try the other one right now!"

I tear my eyes away from the mirror to look at my friends. Surprisingly, they don't look disgusted. Their eyes are almost as wide as their smiles.

"Yeah, we definitely need to see the other one." Otto nods his head in agreement.

Feeling a little bit better about myself, I retreat back into the changing room. I take the green shirt off and fold it, putting it in a mental 'maybe' pile. I struggle a little with putting on the crochet top—the ties in the back are difficult to maneuver. When I finally get it on I step out and look in the mirror.

All I can see is my eczema. The discolored patches covering my shoulders and arms. I look gross and bumpy.

This time, Jessie beats Roxie to hyping me up.

"Cecelia. This looks excellent! You're buying it right?" I turn around to see them staring at me.

"No, it looks awful. Look at my eczema!" I gesture to my shoulders.

"What eczema?" Otto asks, a smile playing on his face.

"It's gross. I look gross."

"No, amiga, you don't." Jessie stands up and takes me by the elbows. "You look beautiful."

Chapter Six

Ninth Grade, February

I have a complicated relationship with routine. In some ways, I love it. I thrive with routines. They make me feel like I'm in control of my life. I follow a rigid schedule and nothing can hurt me. It keeps me safe. Anxiety thrives on uncertainty, so it helps my brain to know exactly what's going to happen and what time. It seems boring, but I need at least a little bit of routine in my life.

However, the routine that I am currently stuck in does not feel safe. It does not make me feel like I'm in control, quite the opposite in fact. When the most consistent thing in your life is

47

that you will, without a doubt, have a panic attack every day. It takes away the sense of control that you need so badly.

I've given up hope on a couple of things in my life. I know that until I get a hold of my declining mental state, I won't be able to make a friend of any sort. It's almost entirely impossible with social and general anxiety disorders.

Speaking of mental disorders, our school has decided it would be a good idea for us to learn about mental illnesses in health class. It's the kind of course that would be helpful for people who have no clue about anything mental illness related, but for those of us who already fucking know everything, it's just another source of stress and discomfort.

Today is the second day of the counselor coming into our class. I already know the counselor quite well, given my situation. On the first day, she just explained what she was going to talk about and what her 'expectations' were for our class. Don't tease, don't be disrespectful, don't joke, etc. So far my peers have not met said expectations.

This version of our health block takes place during the last block on Thursday. By this point, everyone is exhausted and ready for the weekend. Not the best environment to discuss chemical imbalances and SSRIs.

The walls are slowly starting to cave in on me. My turtleneck sweater no longer feels warm and comforting, instead it's suffocating and itchy. I pull on it as if having nothing touching my neck will help me breathe better. **Can't breathe. Can't breathe.** *I feel a million eyes burning holes in the back of my head, but when I turn around, no one is looking.* **Why did you turn around? Stupid. Stupid.**

The counselor has us move the desks to the side so we can stand in a circle. We're gonna do some sort of mindfulness activity. **Can't do it, can't do it.**

The sounds are no longer individual sounds, no longer individual conversations. It's messy muddled microphone feedback taking over my thoughts and rational thinking. All I can think is **get out, get out.**

I walk up to the counselor and tap her on the shoulder, my hands shaking in the air.

"I need to get out here. I can't do this," I tell her. Usually, I'd be embarrassed to freak out in front of someone, but I have other things on my mind. She's also seen me freak out more than a few times.

"It's okay just to stand at the back of the room," she instructs me. I want to argue, but she's already started talking to someone else. **Need to get out.**

Deciding to listen to her instructions, I walk over to the back of the room and press my back against the wall. It hurts my back to stand like this, I'm so used to standing hunched over. I've read that people with anxiety stand like that not only because they're insecure, but also because they're protecting their bodies from potential danger.

I try to focus on the feeling of my back against the wall, but the sounds are too much. They are in my ears, in my head, in my stomach. What would happen if I succumbed to the panic? What would happen if I gave up? I can't figure it out. Some people say that you should ride the wave of panic, but whenever I try, my thoughts drown out any attempt I can make.

Focus on the wall. Focus on the wall. Focus. On. The. Wall.

*I can't. I can't. **I. Can't.***

What are five things I can see?

Um.

Um.

Desk.

Uh.

Chair.

Kid.

Um.

Teacher.

Plant.

*What are four things I can feel? I don't know. I don't know. **I. Don't. Know.** Is it gonna be okay? It has to be okay. It has to be okay. **It's not okay.** I don't think I'm okay. Someone help me. I'm not okay.*

*In the circle, the counselor is handing out marshmallows. The kids have to hold it and focus on how it feels and smells. Now they put it in their mouth and focus on how it feels and tastes. They're all staring. **They are all staring.***

I scan the classroom, trying to restart my 'five senses' exercise.

I'm not alone.

Apparently, I'm not the only one who can't participate in something like this. I'm not the only one who, for whatever reason, needs to have their back against the wall and can't be in the circle.

About ten feet from me, Otto is standing in the exact position I am. He doesn't have a freaked-out look on his face, more like a fake 'fine' one. He looks like he's pretending to be okay. But if someone is okay, they don't tend to need to stand with their back against the wall during mental health activities. That is not a fine person thing. That is a hurt person thing.

I guess I've been staring at him or something because he turns his head to look at me. I look back. I attempt to show a smile of sorts. Something to let him know that it's okay. Something to let him know that I get it. He sort of smiles and stares at the floor.

In an ideal world, I wouldn't stay standing with my back against the wall. I would move, walk towards him, and start a conversation. I would try to distract him from whatever is spiraling in his head by asking about schoolwork or laughing at a teacher.

I guess in an ideal world, I wouldn't be standing with my back against the wall to begin with.

In an ideal world, I would be standing in the circle and see him struggling. When I'd see him struggling, I'd go talk to him. I'd distract him without needing to distract myself.

But this isn't an ideal world. So I stay standing with my back against the wall, trying to be somewhat okay.

Chapter Seven

My eyes dart from outfit to outfit, unable to make a decision. What do I wear? I bought so many new clothes yesterday that I don't even know where to start. Tiny shirts peek out from shopping bags, begging me to put them on. I don't think I can.

Today is the annual Oublie Fair. It's a carnival that takes place on the first Sunday of summer break to celebrate the start of summer. There will be people I know there. Everyone from any town remotely close to ours attends the fair. I don't know how it got decided that we'd be the town hosting, but it's the most epic event that Lake Oublie ever hosts.

My tote bag sits on my desk chair, chock-full of everything I need to make me a little bit less crazy. I've shoved in thousands of fidgets and my anti-anxiety meds, lorazepam.

53

That bag also contains these weird herbal gummies, just in case I'm scared to use my real drugs.

Usually, the crowds freak me out. Usually, I'm not able to function at something like this. Usually, I get stressed out and overwhelmed, and things tend to end with me going home and watching a movie by myself.

At least, they used to.

In ninth grade, we left and went to Jessie's house. It was a little awkward because the four of us had only just started to hang out.

In tenth grade, we left and went to my house to have a sleepover.

Last year we hung out in a park by the beach. Today, I'm determined to stay for the entire thing. I don't want to have to leave because I'm freaked out. I refuse to let that be me anymore.

I decide to wear one of the new dresses I bought shopping yesterday. It's pretty and white and hangs just below my knees. My freckled shoulders are exposed, unlike how they usually would be in a giant sweater. It's a little out of my comfort zone, but what else is this summer for but leaving my comfort zone?

A knock sounds from the door downstairs. We're meeting at my house and then walking to the fair. As you can probably tell, I love to host things. Nobody argues, because they all hate the effort of hosting so we always meet at my house no matter where we're going. Plus, I have all the best snacks.

Roxanne shows up at my house in a red detailed tube top, red bucket hat, and short jean skirt. The confidence it must require to wear something like that is insane. I could never. Her black mesh bag is hanging off one shoulder, random paraphernalia poking out of the holes. Keys, lip gloss, disposable camera, flashlight. Everything you could ever imagine is in that bag, including a bulging wallet.

"Dude, how much money do you have in there?" I ask.

"Seventy bucks in cash."

"Don't lose that thing," I warn, greeting Jessie and Otto as they come inside.

"You guys ready to go?" Jessie questions, looking us up and down to confirm that we have everything that we need.

"Do any of you have sunscreen on?" I raise my eyebrows as they all look at the floor. "Put. It. On." I hand my bottle of sunscreen to them, watching carefully as they apply it.

I know it might not matter now when we're all young or whatever, but three of my relatives died from skin cancer. I can't have any of them die, even if it's really far in the future. We need to become cranky old people together.

I wear my cowboy boots to the fair, not caring that Roxie snorts when she sees them. For some weird reason, they make me confident. It might just be because they make me tall.

The walk to the carnival is only a couple blocks long but it's so hot you could fry an egg on the curb. Roxanne fishes a water bottle out of her bag and takes a long drink. I take the bottle from her and take a huge gulp, handing it to Jessie when I'm done. Otto always keeps his own one-liter water bottle with him, filling it to the brim whenever he has a chance.

When we get to the beach, there are already millions of people here. Rides loom over us like skyscrapers as little kids run around under us. My palms immediately fly to my ears, trying to block out the sound. Jessie puts their hand on my shoulder, letting me know it's okay. I wish my brain knew the difference between real danger and fake danger. For example, big crowds are not a real danger. That's the whole thing with anxiety. My brain doesn't know what's safe and what's not.

I'm safe. Noise isn't dangerous. Noise isn't dangerous.

"Okay, Otto. Kiss, Marry, Kill," Roxanne says, proceeding to name three of their favorite actresses.

"Oh, I'd have to kiss the girl from that superhero movie."

They aren't technically playing 'Kiss', marry, kill. They just say that so I won't get grossed out or get mad at them for objectifying women. I still do both of those things, just in my head.

"Guys." Jessie snaps their fingers in front of their faces. "Tickets are insanely expensive." I look up at the board with the prices. It's one hundred dollars for admission. With that, you can go on any ride you want, but a hundred dollars?! That's insane!

"Y'all I cannot afford this," I tell them. Roxanne gets a sly grin on her face.

"Well, I guess it's time to check off another bucket list item." She pulls out her phone to show us the list. "Sneak in somewhere."

Jessie and I share a worried look. With that glance, I know that both of our anxieties are acting up right now. Getting in trouble is not good for social anxiety. Humiliation and people staring at you are both things that go hand in hand with trouble. I know that breaking rules is cool or whatever, but I'd rather be safe than sorry.

"Do we have to?" I ask, panic shaking my voice. "I don't want to get in trouble."

Jessie nods eagerly at my words, but Roxanne shakes her head.

"Come on, it'll be fun! Didn't you say that you wanted to be able to do this? To face your anxiety and stuff?"

Easy for her to say, she doesn't have it. It's impossible to explain to people that haven't experienced it for themselves.

"Yeah, but that was one thing at a time. I didn't think we would be doing it all at once." I pick at my nail beds, fighting the urge to run far far away.

"Cecelia," Otto speaks up, turning my attention away from the exit. "It's gonna be okay."

"I know but–"

"It'll be okay. If it's too much, we can leave. If we get caught, which we won't, you can blame Roxie. Everyone loves her so she can get away with anything."

His words and tone reassure me a little bit.

You will never be able to do anything.

Nobody likes you.

You ruin all the fun.

I can't let the voices in my head stop me from doing this. The anxious side of my brain takes over every part of my life. It convinces me I'm going to fail or that none of my friends like me. This is the last summer to change that. I'm going to have to do stressful things in university. I'm going to have to face it by myself. There's no other option. I have to do this. I have to.

"Okay fine. Let's do it."

We pass a couple of security guards as we walk around to the back of the carnival. I feel like they're staring at us. **They're staring at you.**

I quiet the voice in my head that wants to object, instead examining the back of Roxanne's head and the way she walks so nonchalantly. Relax.

"Cecelia, go tell that security guard that there's a lost little kid by the outhouses," Roxanne instructs when we reach a part of the fence we can squeeze through.

"What?! Why me?!"

"Exposure therapy."

"Oh my god, you cannot keep using that as an excuse!" I groan but reluctantly make my way over to the security guard.

"Um.. there's a little boy by the outhouses? ...He needs help finding his mom," I stammer, hoping he can't tell that I'm lying.

"And you just left him there? Good job," he mutters and walks off.

HE HATES YOU. It feels like I've just been punched in the stomach. I could easily throw up right now.

I make my way back to my friends, unable to calm the pounding in my chest.

"...Cecelia, are you okay?" Otto asks. "You look like a ghost."

"Gee, thanks," I mumble, attempting to play it off like a joke.

"What happened?" Jessie queries.

"I.... he's mad at me," I whisper.

Otto reaches into my bag, pulls out a stress ball, and hands it to me. "It's okay. He's probably just tired. It's nothing personal. He won't remember you tomorrow, and even if he does, you'll never have to see him again. Okay?"

"Okay." I exhale, repeating his words in my head.

"We good?" Roxanne confirms.

"Yeah," I tell her.

The four of us squeeze ourselves through the crack in the fence. Roxanne goes last, wincing as the fence squeezes her chest.

"Are your boobs too big, Roxie?" Otto laughs.

"That's what your mom told me," she retorts, reaching her hand out for a high five. I give it a weak pat, anxiety still prominent in my stomach.

"Don't we need tickets to go on rides?" Jessie asks. "How are we supposed to do this?"

"We don't need tickets, we need wristbands. We just have to find some wristbands," Roxanne explains. "We each have to find someone who is leaving and ask them for their band. Give 'em ten bucks or something, they don't need it anymore."

"But.... I'd have to talk to someone to do that." Instead of little flutters of nervousness, my stomach feels as if it's been grabbed by a furious sea monster twisting and compressing it.

"Yeah, it'll be good!" Roxanne grins. "Exposure therapy!"

She clearly doesn't know the definition of exposure therapy. You're supposed to slowly expose yourself to things in a comfortable, controlled environment. Not this. This is more than slightly exposed, it's entirely naked and paraded around.

It's terrifying.

You can't do this.

I have to do it. What's it going to be like next year when I have to talk to people to make friends? That won't go well for me. I need to do this now to prove that I can.

"Okay, fine, I'll do it. But someone else has to go first."

Roxanne struts over to a twelve-year-old boy leaving out the gate and taps him on the shoulder. I can't hear what she's saying, but she's got a loop of hair around her finger and is twirling it slightly. Jesus.

The kid drops his wristband on the ground in front of her. Weird. Roxanne picks it up and gallops back to us.

"Roxie, I'm gonna make one thing clear." I sigh. "I will not be flirting with a child to get a wristband."

"That's fine. Just as long as you get one. Go on, my children."

I walk over to the gate, wringing my hands. I have to find a target. I immediately veto any teenagers – that's terrifying. Anyone in their early twenties is also eliminated – they're too close to my age. That narrows the crowd down quite a bit. Most kids are attached to their parents, and that wouldn't work.

My eyes finally land on a couple in their early thirties. The guy is a total golden retriever gamer boy, meaning he'll be quiet and nice. The girl is pregnant and has purple hair, meaning she'll be cool and probably nice as well. I approach them, nervously scratching my arm.

"..Hi... Um," I stutter, trying to remember what I was going to say. "Are you... leaving?"

Idiot. You sound ridiculous.

"Um... yeah." The girl smiles softly.

"I was wondering if you, um, needed to keep your wristband? I-I'll give you money for it if you want some."

Freak.

The guy laughs. "You don't need to pay us. We'll give you one."

His girlfriend unravels her wristband and hands it to me. "There you go, dude."

"Thank you!" I try to give them my kindest smile before running back over to Roxanne.

Weirdo.

I shake my head, attempting to expel the thoughts.

"Did you do it?" Otto asks, walking up behind me.

"Yep! Spoke to people. You can give me a medal now."

"Bravo!" Roxanne cheers. "I knew you could do it."

Jessie arrives, a band in their hands. "Let's do this thing!"

We go on nearly every ride in the park, with the exception of the little kid ones and the ones that made me hyperventilate by looking at them.

Roxanne forces us to go on the zero gravity ride, and I swear I almost shit my pants.

BUT I DID IT!!!

I went on so many scary rides and I survived. It truly boggles the mind.

By the end, I'm so exhausted, I can barely keep my eyes open. We only leave the park when they close all the rides.

I run back to my house, breathless. I can't believe I survived.

Chapter Eight

I slept in until eleven this morning. I don't know how I did it. I haven't slept in that long in forever! I've just been reading for the past hour. It's basically lunch and I'm still in bed. A golden beam is peeking out through my lacy curtains and onto my floral bedsheets. This is my happy place right here.

My mom knocks on my door softly, not sure if I'm awake yet. She slips her head in and smiles when she sees me.

"So, you went to the carnival yesterday?" she confirms.

"Yeah. I stayed there until one a.m!"

"And... how was that?" I guess it's obvious when I'm stressed about things. I've probably been talking about this for months without even realizing it.

"It was fun. A little scary, but fun."

"That's good. I'm glad that you've been able to do stuff like that lately." She smiles and leaves, leaving the door open a crack. I stand up to close it. I don't know why, but I'm never able to focus with my door open. I don't know if it's the sounds, or the extra light source or what. I just can't concentrate.

I eventually became too hungry to keep reading. I make my way downstairs to find something for breakfast. Or is it lunch at this point? It's basically twelve-thirty. I make myself the easiest thing I can think of. A peanut butter and jam sandwich. Classic and simple.

I pull out my phone and scroll through my emails. My boss confirmed the extra shifts I'm picking up at the library. I'm working extra because I have so much free time right now.

I've got five unread texts. One of them is a video that Otto sent me. 'These two people are always best friends' is the caption. It says 'hopeless romantic' and 'never had a crush' are the two people. I'd say that's pretty accurate. I text back with 'lmfao'.

The other four messages are from the group chat. They're trying to make plans to hang out. Jessie is saying that we should go to the beach. Roxanne is saying we should go see a movie. Otto thinks that both of those plans suck, but he can't think of anything better.

I chime in, suggesting we go to the park. Everyone agrees since we haven't been there yet this summer. The park is really just the elementary school. It's got the most amazing playground, complete with zip lines and saucer swings. I'm not even ashamed to say that I love going there. Plus, the field gets sprayed with sprinklers every two hours, which is perfect during the summertime.

I take off yesterday's dress. I didn't mean to sleep in it, but I was too tired to change. I haven't taken a shower in four days, so I'm especially gross right now.

We renovated our shower last year and it's the most amazing thing ever. We got one of those benches you can sit on while showering so my Gido can have one when he comes over, but I tend to just sit on it whenever I'm tired. Which is a lot.

I connect my phone to the shower speaker and blast my summer playlist. As soon as the water hits me, I feel a thousand times better. It's easy to forget about life in a shower. You only have to focus on one thing: getting clean. It's simple and wonderful.

The smell of my vanilla shampoo fills the fogged glass — paradise. I exfoliate with a coconut scrub because it's summer so I need some version of a summer scent. I shave my armpits and legs. My whole legs, not just my shins. Summer glow-up! I want to feel as squeaky clean as humanly possible.

Eventually, I have to get out of the shower. I use my vanilla lotion all over, plus a special cream for my eczema. The special lotion smells like gross medicine, so I spray perfume over the spots where I put it. That's probably not very good for my eczema, but it's fine.

I get dressed in my bathing suit, but cover it up with shorts and an oversized tee. I braid my hair, squeezing the extra water out as I go. Should I wear a hat? I just washed my hair so I don't really want to. I do my morning skincare and some basic makeup. Sunscreen everywhere. I inspect myself in the mirror, looking for anything someone could judge. It sounds pathetic, but I have to make sure. What if I see someone I know from school? I need to make sure that no one would ruin my life over it.

Although, it's summer break. Before university. And... no one else in my class is going to the same university as me. It's the summer of no regrets, right?

I dig a dark green bandana out of the back of my closet. I stopped wearing it when I heard someone say that bandanas were only for cowboys. I don't even remember who it was, yet I haven't worn a bandana since. I wrap it around my head, tie it under my braids, and pull my curtain bangs out so they hang in front of my face.

It's barely anything. It's barely a difference. But it's something. It's a baby step towards not caring. And baby steps are better than no steps at all.

The park is right beside Roxanne's house. It was awesome in elementary school when she could just roll out of bed five minutes before she had to be there. Now, there's a bunch of little kids running by her house daily, so it's a little annoying.

Everyone is already at the park. Jessie and Roxanne are lying down on a picnic blanket, holding hands. Otto is sitting cross-legged beside them.

"Oh thank god, Cecelia!" He leaps up and jogs over to me. "These two have just been talking about their futures for like ten minutes."

I look over at the two of them. As I've said, I love romance stories. Any kind honestly. Rom-coms, romantic tragedies, the whole lot. The only kind I refuse to read is smut because that's not romance to me. Roxanne and Jessie are the ultimate rom-com couple. Perfect opposites attract, grumpy and sunshine, black cat and golden retriever. I could write thousands of stories about characters based on them.

"Race you to the playground?" I say, taking off before Otto can answer.

"No fair!"

I sprint as fast as I can, my feet tumbling over each other underneath me. Otto catches up to me in no time, beating me to the swings by about ten seconds. He puts his fingers in an L above his head.

"Looooser!" he chants, using his feet to boost the swing into the air.

"Ugh fine." I take a seat beside him and lean back to look at the sky. An image pushes its way into my brain, not bothering to consider the circumstances. Me falling backward. Breaking my neck. Not making it out of the hospital. **Dying**. Becoming a part of the sky that my friends would cry to every once in a while. **No one would care.**

I don't know what happens, why my self-control fails me, or why I'm so goddamn sensitive. I break down crying, hating myself for it, and wishing it could be different. Otto looks at me, his eyes full of understanding. He doesn't look scared or weirded out. He should be weirded out. I am a freak.

"Why does it have to be like this?" I whimper, trying to wipe my tear-stained face.

"I don't know dude." He stands up and walks over to me, pushing my back so I sway back and forth in the swing. "Did you get those extra shifts at the library?"

"Yeah. My boss emailed me back this morning. I'm working full days on Wednesdays for the rest of the summer. He even said he'd write a recommendation letter for my application to that bookstore in Montreal."

"That's awesome."

Chapter Nine

Ninth Grade, April

Our school has a huge hockey game against a nearby town today. It's at the rink in between the two towns. It's the last one in the tournament, the one that decides the winner of the whole thing. Everyone in Oublie is going. Even I am going.

The bleachers around the rink are filled to the brim with everyone from toddlers to grannies. It's so fucking loud I can't hear myself think. Except that I can. Because I can always hear myself think. The thoughts scream over the noise.

Too loud.

Too loud.

Too loud!

As I watch the players skate across the ice, I try to focus on my individual senses. If I close my eyes, I can hear the crowd. I can hear the skates scraping against the ice. Scrape. Scraping. Scenarios flood my brain taking over control of my body. Skates scraping my arms and legs. Lying on the ice as someone slits my throat with a blade off their skates. Slitting my own wrists with the blades.

Stop it.

STOP IT.

I can feel the pain of every image. My wrists hurt, my neck hurts. My legs are stinging as if they've been skinned and dipped in vinegar.

I need to go. I need to leave. I can't look at those skates anymore.

*I mumble something about needing air to my mom and rush outside to the concession stands. I stare at the snacks, trying to remember any sort of stress relieving coping strategy. I can't think of any. I need to leave. **Need to leave.***

The crisp April air hits hard the second I step outside. Canadian prairie weather is kind of insane. It snowed last week. Luckily, I'm wearing my coziest sweater and a ridiculously oversized toque. I have to push it away from my eyes constantly.

73

The path home really just consists of weaving through a bunch of '70s houses and empty streets. Literally everyone is at the hockey game. I put my earbuds in and play my spring playlist. It's sort of just a bunch of songs shoved together, like puzzle pieces that don't belong. I don't know how to make it better. I put a bunch of '90s rock songs, with the occasional pop banger. It doesn't work at all. I'm just scared that someone will come across my account and use my music taste against me. I know it's a ridiculous fear, but I can't get it out of the back of my mind whenever I'm making a playlist.

Despite my complicated feelings surrounding my music taste, this playlist actually has some pretty good songs. No one is around, so I spin around while walking, which is the closest thing I can get to dancing. Except, when I turn around, I realize that I'm not actually alone.

I don't know if this is one of those weird coincidences or messages from the universe, but Otto is walking right behind me on the sidewalk. Crap, I just spun around.

Crazy.

Weirdo.

Freak.

Why did I do that?

Insane.

Psycho.

I mean, we all knew that those things about me are true. People that aren't crazy don't have panic attacks. People that aren't freaks don't have to leave hockey games because their intrusive thoughts felt too real.

My face turns bright red and I stare at my feet, counting how many times they land on each square of concrete, and purposely stepping over the cracks. Not that I think it'll break my mother's back or anything, they just feel weird under my feet.

Like I said, **freak**.

The walk feels a thousand times longer now that I know Otto is behind me. I turn off noise canceling on my earbuds so I know where he is. This isn't supposed to happen. He isn't supposed to see me freaking out. He isn't supposed to know that I'm insane until I told him. Until we are the closest friends telling each other everything. Until I am his right-hand man and he is mine. **It isn't supposed to happen like this.**

I guess the mental health talk with the counselor already gave it away. Most people are fine attending that. He wasn't. I guess that's what made it better.

Technically, most people are fine attending hockey games as well. He wasn't. I don't know if that's the case, but it looks like it.

75

I want to ask him. I want so badly to ask him. 'Hey, why aren't you at the game? Did you also leave? Yeah, you did? And... Why is that? Is it a mental illness thing? Are you like me? Would you like to eat lunch with me sometime? I eat in Ms. Wilson's room, what about you?'

That's the thing with my brain. It'll go on and on and on about what I could say. How that conversation would go. Every good scenario and every bad scenario. Especially the bad scenarios.

What kind of thing is that to imagine? What kind of thing is that to daydream about? I've been thinking about this friendship for so long, I have no idea what it would look like if it actually happened. Even if it happened, I could never tell him how long I thought about it. How I used it as an example in therapy for something I wish I could do that anxiety was holding me back from doing.

Let's be real, I don't need to think about that. What would happen if we became friends? It'll never happen. That kinda stuff doesn't happen to people like me. It happens to people who deserve it, people who work for it. Friendships don't just happen.

I finally have to stop walking along this same street. I've got to turn down a road into a little backroad. Just my luck, Otto also turns. A little later, so instead of being right behind me, he's across the street. The road isn't very wide, just enough for one car to fit. It's a bit of a shortcut, only people that live on this road take it. Has he lived on the same street as me my whole life? That's wild.

I keep walking, my brain shouting at me to say something, anything. My eyes stay stuck to the sidewalk, no matter how badly they want to check if he's acknowledged me.

I can't believe I spun around earlier and he was right behind me.

The song that plays through my earbuds next is a whole anthem about going outside of your comfort zone. Pushing boundaries. Whatever. I added this song to my playlist specifically with the intention of reminding myself to make friends. So far it hasn't worked out that well for me.

The end of the road is coming up. It meets with a smaller street to form a sort of T shape. I know he doesn't live on my side of the T because I know every single person in that little cul-de-sac. He's gotta be going the other way.

I have to do something now. This is the perfect opportunity to talk to him. No one else is around. I won't get another chance like this... ever.

My voice feels caught at the back of my throat, but I manage to push a word out, regretting it as I do.

"Bye," I say, waving to him. He turns to look at me, furrows his eyebrows in confusion, and then gives me a sort of half-wave.

So fucking stupid.

Chapter Ten

"I'm not sure I want to do this," I say warily, eyeing the lake off the side of the path. We're walking up, up, up. To the top of a bunch of rocks. A cliff even.

"Come on, we have to! It's on the bucket list!" Roxanne says gleefully, finding humor in my suffering.

"I don't know..." Jessie sighs, shaking their head rapidly. "We're so high up, my intrusive thoughts are having a festival in my brain."

"Amen." I groan.

Jump off. Jump off the cliff. Hit the rocks. What would happen? Who would care?

I can't stop the images of my blood floating around in the lake. I need to... acknowledge the thought. That's what my therapist said.

I am having intrusive thoughts.

A thought is not a fact.

I shiver, wrapping my arms in front of my bikini and grabbing my shoulders. I do not need to listen to every thought that comes into my brain. I do not need to **jump off the cliff.** I do not need to **hit the rocks.**

What is the opposite of that? Stay walking I guess.

Roxanne is scrambling across the rocks giddily like she's been waiting her whole life to do this. She probably has been, honestly.

"Can't we leave this until later?" I beg.

"No! You're on a roll right now! You just broke into a carnival and didn't have to leave because of the crowds! Don't stop while you're ahead."

I don't get the logic behind that. Shouldn't I get a break?

Jump off.

I hate how loud the thoughts get. I hate how sometimes, I actually consider them. I hate how if I tell people about the thoughts, they get worried. I don't want them to be worried. I hate how the thoughts convince me they're real. I hate how I can't get rid of them. I hate how they scare me more than anything.

What is wrong with me? Multiple anxiety diagnoses and yet my biggest fear is myself. What a freak thing.

It's not your fault.

It's your fault.

I hate this.

Jessie locks eyes with me, letting me know that they get it. They get it. It's okay. I'm not alone. I wouldn't call Jessie a freak for having these thoughts, so why should I hate myself? It's different somehow.

I look at Otto, wondering if he feels the same way. By the look on his face, I can tell what he's thinking. One wrong move and it'll all be over. The suffering will be over.

That is the thing that is running through all three of our brains. It makes us sound suicidal, but we're not. At least, not right now. Grade nine was a bad year and I'm not going to say that I wasn't somewhat suicidal then. I'm not there anymore.

I'm not there anymore.

It's just so difficult. Sometimes, life doesn't feel worth it. Sometimes, it does. It all depends on the day, the mood, and the people I'm around.

My thought spiral hits me so abruptly that I almost physically move. So, so, so many pictures. My death. My funeral. My friends sobbing. My friends not caring. My dead mangled body traumatizing them forever. That moment where I'm falling and I know what's about to happen. That moment when I see the rocks nearing closer and I just let myself fall.

I shake my head, the way you do when a bug flies too close to your face. It's a thing I do and a thing Jessie does. Reset your brain so the thoughts go away.

Mental illness, who?

I am a normal teenage girl, climbing rocks with my friends to go cliff jumping. We're going to have an amazing time and I am not going to freak out. Why would I? This is fun.

The edge of the cliff gets nearer and nearer. The air feels thinner up here. Is the air thinner up here? I can't breathe. Holy shit I can't breathe. I'm going to die–

Wait. I'm not actually dying. I'm just freaking out.

I can't breathe.

"Help," I choke, my words quieter than a ghost.

We're on the top of the cliff. Three steps and we fall off the edge. It's about a fifty-foot drop. We're going to jump off in like five seconds.

I can't breathe.

Otto rushes to stand beside me and squeezes my shoulder. We don't have my earbuds. What do I do without my earbuds? Barely louder than a whisper, he starts to speak. But he's speaking with a weird rhythm and strange words. It's almost like...

He's singing a country song. He forgets most of the words so he improvises, sneaking in 'your mom' jokes and the most ridiculous lyrics ever.

But it works. I feel better. My breath is coming back.

"You're gonna be okaaaaay," he sings with a fake twang in his voice. You'd think more of us would have country accents, but we all have Canadian-redneck accents. They're actually very different.

"You okay?" Roxanne's concern covers her face.

"Yeah. Yeah, I think so."

"Cool. We gonna jump?" She gestures to the water below. I know it's safe. People jump off here every day. You just have to go forward, not to the side. It'll be okay.

"...Yeah." I look around at the others. Otto grins and nods his head in agreement. Jessie shivers a bit but smiles.

We grab hands and back up slightly.

"Three...."

My stomach is doing a thousand somersaults per second. I feel like I'm gonna throw up.

"Two....."

Oh no. Big mistake. Nonononononono–

"One!"

I have no time to stop before we take off running. With Roxanne's hand in mine and Otto's in my other, I don't have a chance to chicken out. They're squeezing tightly, either in fear or to make sure I don't run away. Very likely a mix of both.

The edge of the cliff is approaching way too rapidly until it's suddenly not there anymore. The edge isn't there anymore, there is only air. And we're falling.

I let out the most ear-piercing scream on the way down. I let go of the other's hands and flail my limbs around in the air hopelessly as if I'll suddenly gain the ability to fly before we hit the water.

We hit the water.

The first thought that registers is 'ow'. And then 'I did it!' and then 'fuck my bathing suit top came off.'

That's a lot of emotions to go through in the span of three seconds. After coming up for air, I turn around to tie my top back up. I'm wearing board shorts, but I didn't plan to wear my sportier top. I opted for the bikini, not considering the fact that it might fall off.

After properly securing the ties in place, I swim over to the others.

"Dude! We did it!" Jessie whoops.

"And we didn't even die!"

"Crazy!"

Roxanne pops up beside us, looking way too graceful for someone who just went flying off a cliff. "See, was that so hard?" She grins.

"Absolutely. That was one of the most terrifying things I've ever done," I decide.

"Come on, it wasn't that bad! We should go again! It was awesome!" She beams.

Otto swims up from behind me and splashes her in the face. "I SWEAR TO GOD ROXANNE!"

Chapter Eleven

The beach is filled to the brim with people, but we stay anyway. Cliff jumping gave me a temporary confidence boost, so I'm not really concerned with other people right now.

That's a lie. I'm always concerned with other people. I'm just a little less concerned right now. Best I can hope for honestly.

I think Roxanne is sun tanning on the shore. She might just be napping though. Sometimes it's hard to tell when someone is wearing sunglasses. Jessie was the only one smart enough to bring a towel, but of course, they gave it to Roxanne the second she announced she forgot.

Jessie is reading on the sand beside her. They covered their bathing suit up immediately, hating how unnecessarily gendered it is.

Otto and I are doing handstand competitions. At least, we were doing handstand competitions until we got distracted. Now we're just kinda sitting in the shallow water talking.

"I'm really scared of going to college," I tell him. "I'm not going to know anyone."

"You'll make friends," he assures me. "Everyone makes friends in college."

"Typically everyone makes friends in middle school as well." I tilt back in the water, letting it drown out the noise and seep into my hair. It washes away the tension in my neck, leaving only a cool soothed feeling.

Otto taps on my shoulder so I sit up. "Bro. Listen. It's gonna be different now. You're so much better now, cut yourself some slack."

I shake my head and try to stop myself from crying. "I'm only better because I've got you guys. When you're gone, I'm going to go back to square one. I won't have anything."

"Dude. No. You gotta understand, you did this on your own. We had nothing to do with it. You'll be fine."

I don't believe him. I hear the words, but I don't believe them. How am I supposed to believe that, when I only started to get better when they came into my life? What does that mean for me? Am I not a person on my own?

No.

I don't tell him any of this. I just nod my head and smile. I don't want to worry anyone. I've heard saying things out loud makes them true. It's true either way, but I could use any help I can get.

"Okay, rate my handstand!" he says, swimming under the tide and doing a mediocre handstand at best.

"Six," I tell him as he resurfaces.

"What?! Come on, that was better than a six!" he complains, splashing me with water. I shake my head and dive underwater. My hands meet the soft wet sand at the bottom and root themselves in. I keep my legs stuck together and extend them above the surface. I even point my toes. I hold the stance for a good five seconds before coming back up for air.

"Three," he scoffs. I push him over so he falls under the waves.

When I look back at the shore, Jessie is waving us over so we head back to the towel.

"What's up?" I ask.

"Do y'all wanna go get ice cream?" Roxanne asks. There's an ice cream shoppe right beside the beach. It's absolutely incredible. They have forty-nine flavors plus a bunch of sundaes and shakes.

"Absolutely I do." I grin and start to jog over to the shoppe. The rest of them trail behind me, slightly slower.

The air inside the shoppe is way colder than it is outside. I feel like I just stepped inside the actual ice cream freezer. Goosebumps immediately form all over my body.

The other three enter and Otto shivers so much he physically moves.

"I'm gonna wait outside," he tells us.

"Okay, hear me out," Jessie says, gesturing to the menu. "What if we got the epic sundae?"

"Really?" The epic sundae has six different types of ice cream piled on top of each other. There are eight toppings and two syrups, plus a hefty amount of whipped cream. If you eat the entire sundae, you get it for free.

"We definitely have to do that," Roxanne exclaims. "I'll add it to the bucket list right now!"

"Okay, you guys go get a table outside, I'll buy it." I gesture outside, where picnic benches line the grass.

The line moves quickly, giving me barely any time to recite the order in my head. One epic sundae, please. Hi, can I get one epic sundae, please? Yeah, that seems about right.

Going to fail. Going to be embarrassed.

That's not helping.

"Hi, can I get one epic sundae please?" I request. I place a ten-dollar bill on the counter because that requires the least amount of talking.

"Wow, one all to yourself?" Darryl remarks. He's a good friend of my grandpa's. He and Muriel are cousins. Again, everyone is connected somehow.

I don't really reply to him, just smile slightly. If I explain that my friends are outside, he'll ask who. Then when I tell him, he'll inquire about their families and how they're doing. Then he'll act kinda weird about Jessie and Roxanne and their obviously queer relationship. Then he'll give Otto a strange look and ask about his life in a painful sympathetic way. It's weird and just too much socializing for one day.

I watch him as he scoops ice cream into a large metal dish. Chocolate, vanilla, mint chip, caramel, cookies and cream, Moose Tracks. Then the toppings. All of my teeth are going to fall out. Finally, the sauces and finally the whipped cream. With a cherry on top, obviously. He gives me one spoon, but I take three more for the others.

Jesus, I forgot how hot it is outside. The ice cream immediately looks as though it's starting to soften.

Luckily, they picked a picnic table under the shade of a tree. I set the bucket down in the center and take a seat beside Otto.

"What the fuck is this?" Otto asks, peering into the bucket.

"An epic. Freaking. Sundae!" Roxanne exclaims, pulling out her disposable camera for a photo. I take it from her and take a picture of the three of them and the ice cream. Roxanne is ecstatic, Jessie is worried and Otto is laughing. Pretty accurate representation of all of their personalities.

I pass them each a spoon and start to count down.

"Three, two, one, go!"

Roxanne and I both dig in immediately, while Jessie takes little spoonfuls. Otto sets his spoon down and laughs at us.

"You guys look ridiculous." He guffaws. "Roxie, you've got whip cream on your nose."

"Thank you," she mumbles through a mouthful. She doesn't even try to get it off.

I pick Otto's spoon up and get him a little pile of strawberries. I put it down in front of him and then get back to devouring the mint chip part of the ice cream. He takes little bites of strawberries and sighs.

Eventually, Jessie gives up. They put their head down on the table and groan.

"I can't watch you guys eat that anymore."

Roxanne is obviously starting to struggle, but I keep going. She sits back on the bench and sighs.

"You keep going, I'm done."

Otto helps out by scooping up the remainder of the fruit but stops when it's gone.

I can't eat anymore, but there are still at least two scoops of ice cream left in the bucket.

"Oh well, we tried our best." I sigh, standing up. I take the bucket back in and put it in the dirty dishes bucket.

"How'd you do?" Daryl asks, looking at it. "You know, for one person, that's pretty good. I'll give it to you for free." He beams and hands me my ten dollars back.

I'm not going to argue with that.

Chapter Twelve

Ninth Grade, June

Another day. Another morning panic attack. Another hour of wallowing in self-pity before school starts. What a life. One day they'll write books about me and wonder why I didn't kill myself. I wonder the same thing every day. Why do I wake up and face life again and again? I honestly don't know, but I talked to Otto.

Granted, that was only once. And it was two months ago. Somehow, that's enough to keep me going to school. The possibility that I could have started something. I could have started a friendship. Every day, that's the one thing I keep in mind while dragging my feet to the prison-like hell that is the ninth grade.

93

Roxanne is particularly chatty this morning. She is practically bouncing up and down, giggling like a little girl. I say that in the least misogynistic way possible.

"Guess what?" She beams.

"What?" I sigh, not wanting to participate whilst also not wanting to bring her mood down. It's a difficult line to walk.

"I asked Jessie out!" she gushes. My ears perk up and I hate myself for it. Can I only be happy for my friend when there's something in it for me? **Awful person. Selfish.** *I know, I know, I know. I don't deserve any friends. Not Roxanne and definitely not Otto, if I ever managed to talk to him.*

"That's amazing!" I tell her, trying to mask the self-hatred I so prominently feel. "What did they say?"

Worthless, terrible person.

"Yes!" she replies. "We're going out this weekend!"

"Dude, that's incredible."

She grins to herself, likely imagining the perfect relationship in their perfect lives to make a perfectly happy couple forevermore.

"I meant to ask you..." she remembers, distracting my mind from thinking about how everyone is happier than me and then hating myself for pitying myself. It's an endless cycle.

"Where do you go for lunch? I've never seen you in the cafeteria, like at all."

"Oh... I always go to Miss Wilson's room." I look down at my feet. I can't deal with the pitying looks that come with being a teenager with no friends. I get enough of them from my parents.

"You get to go in her room by yourself?! That's dope. Could I join you sometime?"

Huh. That's not what I was expecting. "Yeah, of course. It's not that fun, we just discuss books." I don't tell her the truth about my lunchtime escape. That it's actually my favorite part of my day. The only time when I feel like a real person who can actually maintain a conversation.

"Oh, amazing! The cafeteria is the loudest, most unpleasant place on the face of the earth. If I could never go there again, I would die a happy human."

If only it were that easy to die happy. I guess when you're dead, it doesn't really matter if you were happy beforehand. That's something I have to remember sometimes. I get scared that one day I'll just snap and kill myself. To know that my unhappiness wouldn't matter after that is comforting.

Stop. Stop thinking that. Death is not the only option for getting my happiness back. I have other ways. I am not hopeless. I am going to be okay.

Everything is fine.

***

Lunch comes slower than usual. I know that Roxanne might not come today, but it's nice to imagine. The only trouble is that waiting and wondering if she'll come only makes the time go slower. It's nearly impossible.

I try to distract my brain in any way possible. Recite songs in my head. Write down my biggest desires in life.

I want to go home. I want to go home. I want to go home.

Eventually and reliably, lunch arrives. After what feels like a year of waiting, it arrives.

For lunch today, I have a ridiculous ham and cheese sandwich and a granola bar. I haven't been able to make anything else lately. I've found my eating habits going to shit, fruit and vegetables completely disappeared from my lunches.

I don't know why, but it freaks me out to make my lunch. It might be because I'm preparing for the school day which

96

is terrifying. It might be because there are too many decisions to make and I have no idea what to do.

It doesn't matter. The point is that my lunches have been suffering because the only thing my brain can wrap itself around is a basic dry sandwich and a disgusting granola bar.

I set up lunch at my favorite desk, the one with inspirational quotes engraved into it instead of penises. It makes for an overall more enjoyable dining experience. This desk is also closest to Miss Wilson's desk, so I don't have to yell all the way across the room to have conversations with her. I place my book beside me in case of emergencies.

"What'cha reading?" she asks, gesturing towards my brick of a novel.

"Autobiography from a famous writer. I'm hoping it will somehow teach me how to become a bestseller."

"Best of luck to you in that area." She exhales through her mouth and shakes her head. She told me once that she tried to get published but couldn't get an agent. I'm hoping to self-publish one day so I don't have that problem.

"Thanks. How about you? What're you reading?" I wonder.

"Heh not much, it's just a silly romance–" She is interrupted by someone knocking on the door and laughing outside. *"That's weird,"* she puzzles.

"Oh, that might be me. I invited a friend to eat here. I hope that's okay?"

"Yeah of course!" Her face brightens. I'm sure she knows I don't have many, if any, friends so this is all news to her.

I stand up to open the door to let Roxanne in. Except that, it's not only Roxanne. It's also Jessie. And Otto.

That's okay. I'm not freaking out. I can deal with a change of plans. I can deal with Otto, the person I most want to be friends with, showing up randomly in my safe space in the school. I can deal with small talk and smiles. I can deal with making new friends.

No control. No control.

Maybe I can't.

I stand by the door for a second as Jessie and Otto pull out chairs.

"You wanted to be friends with him, didn't you?" Roxanne mutters to me.

"Yeah, but I wasn't expecting it to be this soon!" I hiss.

"You've been talking about this for six months. It's getting ridiculous. Just say hi." She rolls her eyes as my stomach rolls all over itself inside me.

"Hi guys," I say weakly, sitting back down in my spot. Not knowing what to do, I look at their lunches. Roxanne has delicious-looking Samosas, very likely made by her Nani. Jessie has what looks like leftover pancakes drowned in maple syrup. Otto doesn't have anything.

"You don't have lunch?" I remark.

"No," he says quickly. *"So why do you get to stay here?"*

He hates you.

"I don't know honestly. I just asked one day and I've been doing it ever since." I close my eyes and try to focus on my feet on the floor.

"Cool."

"Yeah. Pretty cool."

Chapter Thirteen

"Okay, what do we do next from the bucket list?" Jessie asks, scrolling through Roxanne's phone.

"I personally think we should do the wedding," Otto suggests, reading over Jessie's shoulder.

"How? We don't know anyone that's getting married." I rack my brain for any wedding announcements, but none come to mind. We tend to know every time someone's getting married. It'll be the talk of the town for a couple of months, at least until someone either dies or gets knocked up. The latter is particularly scandalous.

"Well, I actually had an idea for that one." Roxanne grins and falls to her knee in front of Jessie. She pulls a ring pop out of her pocket and presents it to them. Otto and I gasp dramatically at the same time, as if on cue.

"Jessie Diaz," she recites dramatically. "Will you do me the honor of being my not-so-lawfully wed spouse? I bought cheap promise rings from the dollar store; will you fake-marry me?"

"Say yes!" I shout, covering my mouth immediately afterward. Oops.

"Yes! A thousand times yes!" Jessie covers their face like a blushing bride and takes the ring pop from Roxanne's hands.

I turn to Otto, my brain churning with a million ideas. "Dude. We have to start planning!"

He and I decide to go to the florist first. Roxanne and Jessie go back to their houses to get ready. As it turns out, flowers are incredibly expensive. It's like thirty dollars for one bouquet, and for what? To use them one time and then throw them away?

"Should we just pick some wildflowers and pretend like we bought them?" I whisper so the florist won't hear us.

"Yeah, I think that's a good idea."

We leave the florist.

Our next stop is the bakery. In our minds, we get a beautiful wedding cake. The kind with multiple tiers and the little wax people on top. In reality, that's not very possible.

Apparently, wedding cakes are also incredibly expensive. How do people have weddings and not be immediately broke after?

We leave the bakery.

On the same block as the bakery is a toy store. It isn't your typical toy store with popular brands and dress-up costumes. This toy store is run by an old dude who makes mini things out of wood and sells them. I have, like, forty from when I was little.

"I have an idea," I announce.

"What?" Otto follows my gaze to the store. "This can't be good."

"Hear me out. We bake a cake and buy some mini people to put on top."

"From Norman's?"

"Yeah, they're super cheap. I bet he has some that look just like them."

I was right. We found a little dark-haired girl in a black dress and an androgynous looking blonde one in a white suit.

We buy them instantly and leave the toy store.

"Okay, where do we go now?" Otto asks.

"For sure we have to go to the thrift shop. We've gotta find outfits for everyone."

The thrift store is giant and crowded and smells like old fabric. The lights are cool white and the aisles are just a little bit too small and there are stains on so many of the clothes. It freaks me out that I don't know where those stains come from. I don't like this.

Otto's excitement takes over my panic. He immediately goes to the formal section and pulls out the most ridiculous prom dress, very likely from the nineties.

"Brooo, you gotta get this!" He shouts, scaring an old lady away.

"Fuck no that's disgusting!" I skim through the racks and racks of clothes, pulling out anything hilarious I find. I come across a powder blue suit with a ruffled shirt underneath.

"Yooooo!" I pass it to Otto. He takes it from me and examines it.

"Well, I definitely have to get this. It's my size and everything."

Wow, I was expecting a lot more resistance. His face brightens and he dives back into the racks. He emerges with a cheesy bridesmaid's dress the exact same color as the suit.

"These must have been from the same wedding," I remark, taking it from him.

"They are the perfect outfits for the best man and maid of honor at this wedding!"

The two outfits immediately go into our shopping cart.

"Do we have to find a dress for Roxanne and a suit for Jessie?" I ask, examining some old wedding dresses.

"Yeah, but Roxanne wants a black dress instead of a white one."

"Won't it look like she's going to a funeral?" To this question, he just shrugs.

Hidden behind the frilly white dresses is a beautiful black satin gown. I can't believe someone brought it in here when they could've sold it online for a lot of money.

"Dude, isn't this perfect?" I show the dress to Otto, who puts it in the cart instantly.

"Now for a suit."

The men's formalwear part of the thrift store is a lot more sparse than the dress section.

"Okay, which of these is the most feminine?" Otto asks, showing me three white tuxedos. One is too basic, one is too flamboyant, but one is just right. It's got a gold lining around the coat jacket and dope flared pants. It's not something that someone should wear to a real wedding, but it's perfect for a strange fake wedding.

It goes into the cart instantly.

The lady working the till looks at us weirdly as we give her our items.

"Is someone getting married, Cecelia?" she asks. "I didn't think there were any weddings going on right now. Are you buying outfits for the whole party?" It is extremely uncommon for a wedding to happen and to have someone who doesn't know about it. That just doesn't happen in Lake Oublie.

"Not really," I tell her, shocked when I actually talk. I think she's in her twenties, which isn't an easy kind of person for me to talk to. I get along better with people who are way older than me. It's a lot harder to communicate when someone is sort of close to my age. Older people don't judge you, but young people do. That's just facts.

We rush home and instantly get dressed. Luckily, I happen to have nail polish and eyeliner in the exact same color as our outfits. We do our nails to match and we attempt to do eyeliner, but it just ends up weird and smudgy. Good enough.

We look amazing, so we obviously have to take a couple of mirror selfies before we start to bake.

On second thought, we should've baked the cake before we got dressed.

"Hey, Cecelia. Heads up!"

I turn around just in time to see a handful of flour flying at my face and landing on my dress.

"Otto. You did not just do that." I gasp. "My dress!"

"Oops," he giggles.

"I am going to kill you!" I grab a handful of flour and pelt it at him, hitting him in the chest.

"Hey! We have to bake. Stop acting like a child." He rolls his eyes.

I let out the most dramatic sigh, but get back to baking. I make the batter and he makes the icing. I learn about halfway through that I am not good at baking cakes. Otto learns at about the same point that he is excellent at making icing.

"We should switch jobs," I say.

"Fuck no. You should just be better."

I groan and start pouring the batter into the pans. I think I remembered to grease the pans?

Into the oven it goes. Otto starts playing music that's similar to the sort a middle-aged dad would listen to. He sings every word passionately, using a spatula as a microphone. I roll my eyes, but end up singing along as I'm doing the dishes.

***

The cake is finished. It's sloppy and the icing is sort of melted, but we did it. The little wooden people are placed on top and many, many photos are taken.

After we're done with the cake, we take Roxanne and Jessie's outfits and go drop them off at their houses. Otto is going to help Jessie get ready while I help Roxanne.

Roxanne steps out of her door and runs up to me before I even start up the front stairs.

"Hey, can I get ready at your house? My mom is sleeping, and I don't want to disturb her," she says.

"Oh yeah, of course."

Once we get back to my house, she begs to see the dress. When I remove it from the bag, I swear her jaw drops to the floor.

"Do you like it?" I ask.

"I LOVE it!" she shouts, grabbing it out of my hands. "Oh my god, I'm putting this on right now."

She runs to the bathroom and returns, absolutely glowing.

"Bro, you look so good." I gasp.

"Thank you! I feel so good."

I don't really need to help her much with her hair or makeup; she does a perfect half up half down hairstyle like she's done it a million times before. She keeps her regular daily makeup on, the only change she makes being her lipstick. She looks incredible.

"Are you ready?" I ask once she's done with her makeup.

"Yeah. Are the others ready?"

I text them to make sure and Otto replies with a thumbs up emoji.

They're ready. We're ready. The cake is ready. I've picked a bunch of flowers, half of which might be weeds.

We decided to have the 'ceremony' by the lake. Not in front of everyone, but a little off to the side where no one can see us. It's by where we usually sit, just behind a fallen tree and shaded by some branches. It's the perfect spot for a wedding. We don't really have an officiant, so Otto and I are trading off lines.

"Do you Roxanne Devi take Jessie Diaz to be your not-so lawfully wedded spouse, until university do you part? Or death, if you meet up again later in life." I say, adding the last part so it doesn't sound like I'm rooting against them.

"I do."

"And do you Jessie Diaz take Roxanne Devi to be your not-so lawfully wedded wife until university do you part?"

"I do."

"You may now kiss each other!" he and I yell at the same time.

They kiss and then immediately run into the lake. That's a good idea, it's freaking boiling out here. We splash around in the water, our ridiculous outfits getting drowned by the waves.

I wrap the two of them up in a hug, trying my best to stay above the surface. I start to shout, scaring a couple of kids around us. "You guys are going to have the hottest children!"

Chapter Fourteen

I haven't left my house in the three days since the wedding. To be honest, I haven't really left my bed. I've been watching TV shows and eating chips and literally nothing else. I've tried to write a bit, I promise I have, but it didn't work. Words just won't come to my brain.

I feel like I should be sad about something. There's something deep inside me that is mourning something, but I don't know what it is.

I think it might be my childhood. I don't know anything other than school. I've been in this town, in this house for my whole life. What's it gonna be like when I randomly move to Montreal and stay in dorm rooms? Am I going to be okay?

I wish I didn't have to grow up. As much as I want to make money, live on my own, and start a family — adopting kids would be so incredible — I'm terrified. I can't remember a time when I couldn't just talk to my parents or Roxanne. I've been at my lowest, always wanting to go to sleep and never wake up, but I had my family the entire time. Even in these most recent years, Jessie and Otto have become part of what I consider my family. I'm not ready to leave them. Shit, I'm mourning something I haven't even lost yet.

I keep trying to pick up my phone and reach out to someone. Ask them to hang out. Anything to get my mind off my impending doom. I just haven't been able to. If someone messages the group chat, I'll hang out with them, but until then, I just need to sit here watching TV for a bit.

***

Someone does indeed message the group chat. It's Otto. He's asking which bucket list item we're checking off next. Roxanne is typing back.

'Skinny dipping.'

Seriously? I thought we'd pick an easy one! This is not easy! My mental state is not stable enough for this right now.

'Are you sure?' I type back. 'Can't we do an easy one?'

To that, she sends a GIF of someone shaking their head.

Well, crap. Do I really want to leave my cozy perfect bed to go swimming in the lake naked? Not really.

'What time?' I ask.

'10'.

Okay, so that's like seven hours. In that time, I can take a nap, and eat dinner..... I don't know. Do nothing, really. Stay in bed? That's the ideal option but not the best one for my 'mental health'.

I don't have a lot of time to mull over that thought, because someone rings the doorbell down the hall. Both of my parents work, so I'm the only one at home. I pad down the hallway in my pajamas, not caring that they have penguins on them and a couple of holes.

Otto is standing outside, an iced tea in his hands.

"Hey bro," I greet. "What're you doing here? I thought we were hanging out at ten?"

"Yeah, but I was bored. Wanna watch movies?"

I guess it's somewhat better than watching mindless reality shows on my own.

"Sure. What do you want to watch?" I ask as we make our way downstairs.

"We could rent that new movie that's based on a video game?" He suggests.

I wrinkle my nose. "Isn't that like a car racing movie?"

"Fine. Not that one. What do you want to watch?" he sighs.

"There's a really good rom-com you haven't watched yet! It has an excellent scene in a library. Plus, it's gay."

"Cecelia, I say this in the nicest way. That sounds like something you should watch with Jessie, not me."

"Ugh." I flop back onto the couch. "Should we just watch them again?" I say, referring to our favorite superhero trilogy. It's got the perfect balance of romance and action to keep us both entertained.

"I think it's our only option at this point."

I hit play on the movie and we immediately start to discuss the same topics we've discussed for the past four years. We know the movies so well we don't even have to watch them anymore.

"If you could have any superpower, what would it be?" He asks, knowing my answer. I'll say teleportation and he'll say invisibility. Guaranteed, every time.

"Teleportation."

"Yeah. I'd wanna be invisible. It would make tonight a lot easier," he snorts.

Tonight. Skinny dipping. Even though neither of us explicitly say so, I know that we're both terrified.

"Don't you wish we could live in this world?" He groans, staring at the TV.

"Yeah."

It's a tragedy that I was born into this world. I like to think that I'd be happier in a different universe. It's a somewhat comforting thought.

***

By the time we're finished watching our movies, it's already nine-thirty. Basically, time to go.

I'm not scared of walking around after dark anymore. I used to be constantly thinking that someone was gonna jump out and attack me. I have since learned that nothing like that happens in Oublie. The last time someone went missing was ten years ago, and it turned out that they just ran away. It was dreadfully uneventful.

The beach is empty for the first time in a couple of months. There's no one on it except for Roxanne and Jessie. The moon reflects onto the tide and it's the most beautiful thing I've ever seen. If I could freeze time, I'd freeze it here. On the edge of a beach, in the dark, surrounded by my favorite people. If I never had to leave, I never would.

Roxanne runs up to us and starts to yell. "Come on! Are y'all ready for this?"

Otto and I share a look that says we are definitely not ready for this. For him, clothes are his safety net. He can layer and layer them and cover up the parts of himself he can't look at. No one calls him 'sick' in his baggy hoodie. Humans don't notice the pain until it's right under their eyes.

By the look on their face, clothes do a similar thing for Jessie. Cover up the parts they don't want anyone to see, including themselves. The parts that make the world see them as a certain sex, a certain role in society.

Roxanne starts to undress and runs into the waves. I wish I knew how she has the confidence to do everything first.

As for me, clothes are my barrier. They're my reliable source.

I know exactly how each item in my closet feels on my skin and how each one makes me feel. Clothes are safe. After all, they were designed to keep people safe.

Jessie goes next. They slowly remove their clothes, wading underwater to cover their body.

People may say that skinny dipping is just something to use as a stupid dare, but it's more than that. It's showing people that you're comfortable with them, that you don't need a safety net. It's going outside of your box to prove something to yourself. It's an extreme vulnerability. It's the perfect thing to fix everything wrong with my brain.

It's terrifying and I'm almost ready to go home, but I don't. I submerge myself in the water and relax. Finally, relax. Feeling the water on my back is the most wonderful feeling. It's like I'm bathing in nature.

Otto is the last to make it into the lake. Even though it's too dark to see, none of us look at him, giving him the space he needs. His mind warps his view of his body, telling him that everything looks wrong.

"This was an amazing idea," I tell Roxanne in the darkness.

"It's not me, it's the summer," she says.

There's a moment of silence as we all consider that.

Otto is the first to start laughing. "That was the cheesiest fucking thing you've said in your entire life."

The rest of us crack up, the tension dissolving under the surf.

We start to paddle back to shore, a fulfilled feeling settling in my chest. When we reach the shore, Jessie starts counting down.

"Three.... two... one.....run!" They take off for the forest, a towel in one hand and Roxanne's clothes in the other. After grabbing our towels, Otto and I follow them to the bench where they've sat down.

I'm entirely sure that Roxanne's shouting wakes up the entire town. "FUCK YOU GUYS!!!!"

Chapter Fifteen

Tenth Grade, October

There's something off about Otto's girlfriend, Gail. All of us think so. We could never tell him that though; he's so incredibly in love with her that he can't see any of her flaws. And she has many flaws.

Roxanne, Jessie, Otto, and I spent all summer together. We spent all summer together, except for when Gail would call Otto, insisting he quit all his plans to hang out with her. She makes him feel special, praising his art and telling him he's incredible.

The thing is, she doesn't know anything. They've been dating for six months, and yet she keeps trying to force him to eat. She doesn't understand.

We've been having sleepovers every Friday night at my house. I invited Gail once, but never again after that. She spent the entire night trash-talking people at our school, people that are obviously struggling.

That's not all though. She found out that Jessie and Roxanne are lesbians and acted really confused.

"But like, you're not real lesbians," she said. She had taken out her phone and started to text her friends. I peeked over her shoulder to see what she was writing, but all I caught was the word 'dyke'. I haven't told anyone.

Later that night, when we were eating pizza, Roxanne reached for a second slice and Gail wrinkled her nose, asking if 'she was sure she wanted to eat all that'. Meanwhile I was helping myself to a third.

And then Jessie and I started to talk about anxiety and how we were scared for school, she laughed at us and changed the topic. It was awful. It's stuff like that that reminds you you're not supposed to be like this. Normal people aren't supposed to be like this. It inconveniences other people when we open up. Jessie and I spent the rest of the night barely speaking a word. It sucked.

Otto only sees her strengths. He sees her comforting him when he fails a test or buying him flowers when he's sick. All very nice gestures, but when emotions go beyond the normal everyday stuff, she shuts down.

It's Friday night, so we're having a sleepover, as usual. Otto's going to be a bit late, he's going out with Gail for a while.

"So, I've been thinking," Roxanne announces, pulling us out of the movie we've been watching. "We obviously need to get rid of Gail. I've got a plan."

"I'm gonna stop you right there." Jessie pauses the movie and turns to look Roxie in the eyes. "Mi amor, I know you want to help him. Trust me, I do too. But we can't meddle in his life. He's his own person, we can't make decisions for him. That's not our job."

"Yeah yeah, I know." She rolls her eyes. "However, my idea is that we try to make her look bad in front of him so he realizes how much she sucks. We'll discuss mental illness and homosexuality until she snaps and then Otto will have to break up with her! It's foolproof."

"Roxie–" Jessie starts, but I cut them off before they get a chance to finish.

"I don't think that'll matter very much," I say cautiously, staring out the window. Underneath a blanket of

pouring rain, Otto's shape is vaguely visible. He's running and wiping his face. He wasn't supposed to get back from hanging out with Gail for another hour.

Something is wrong.

I run up to the door before he gets there. I tell Roxie and Jessie to stay downstairs. Jessie is reluctant, but they agree.

I open the door and let Otto in. I wrap him in a hug, ignoring my discomfort around physical touch for just a bit. His entire body is shaking from either the cold or sobs. Likely both. He's not wearing a coat, only his signature hoodie, which is soaked all the way through.

"It's okay," I tell him. "It'll be okay." I don't know what it is, or if it will, in fact, be okay. All I know is that is what he needs to hear right now.

"She broke up with me," he chokes, tears staining his cheeks.

"Oh fuck, Otto. I'm sorry. Just breathe. Want to go downstairs or stay here?"

"Downstairs." His voice is thick and deep, the way it sounds when he's at his lowest. I've only heard it this way once before, during the late hours of a sleepover while we were discussing not wanting to be alive. I really, really hope he's not thinking that right now.

121

I grab him a fluffy blanket as we make our way downstairs. Jessie and Roxanne understand immediately. He sits down beside them and stares at the TV, his eyes betraying the rest of his face with a glimpse into his shattered heart.

I hate Gail.

Roxanne grabs him an extra pair of clothes from her bag, an oversized shirt and sweatpants. He goes to the guest room to change. It's the only room down here without a mirror. I don't want him to analyze the way he looks right now.

"She broke up with him," I mutter after he leaves.

"I'm going to fucking kill her," Roxanne says, her voice dripping with anger.

"Querido Otto," Jessie whispers.

The thing is, this is so much more than a regular breakup. Gail has been everything to Otto. Everything he did, he did for her. His entire worth was based on what she thought of him. What does that mean for him now?

He emerges from the bathroom, his wet clothes bundled up in his arms.

"Where should I put these?" he asks.

"Here, I'll take them." I hang them up in the bathroom, trying not to cry when I realize he was wearing three shirts under his hoodie. He must've been so cold.

He sits back down on the couch and bundled himself up in blankets. Roxanne has changed the movie to his comfort film, an extraordinarily well-directed piece on the personal life of a struggling superhero. An interesting plot, but he sees himself in the protagonist. That's what he's told us.

Suddenly, he speaks. "I didn't mean for this to happen. I didn't. I should've just — I should've just stayed quiet. I didn't mean for her to hear, I didn't mean..." He trails off, staring at the screen.

"Otto." I put my arm on his shoulder so he looks at me. "What did you say?"

"I... told her I didn't want to be alive sometimes. We were watching a movie... and the character tried to kill himself so I told her I related to him. I told her that life is so terrifying that I don't want to be here sometimes and she..."

"What did she say?" Jessie says, looking at him, then locking eyes with me.

"She said that I can't expect her to be my psychologist. That it's too difficult for her to date me. That I'm a freak, just like all my friends. And then she broke up with me."

No.

It's hard enough to be open with someone you love about mental illness. To admit that life feels harder for you and that you don't know if you'll ever be okay.

How could she? How could she do that to him?

"It wasn't your fault," Roxanne speaks up. "It wasn't your fault. You can't control that kind of thing."

"I shouldn't have told her. Why did I put that on her?"

We hear the words he doesn't say. How he doesn't think anyone could ever love him. How he's too difficult for everyone. We know, because we've thought the same things.

"I'm so sorry Otto," I tell him. "You didn't deserve that. You didn't deserve any of that."

Chapter Sixteen

"It's time for the next phase of our plan," Roxanne decides in the middle of Friday movie night.

"What plan?" I wonder, racking my brain for any huge plans we've made in the past month.

"The whole 'facing our fears/becoming cooler people' plan."

"I didn't know that was an official plan. I thought it was just a bucket list," Otto says.

"Well it is a bucket list, but the list is a part of the plan! Stop ruining it!" she whines.

"Okay fine, sorry," I sigh. "What's the next phase?"

"Getting revenge."

"...Huh?"

"Who are we getting revenge on? I feel like everyone is pretty chill," Jessie muses.

"I believe you're forgetting about the she-devil. The name to never be spoken." Roxanne waves her hands around dramatically.

"Roxie, we don't have to get revenge on Gail. That was years ago." Otto sighs.

"What part of 'never to be spoken' do you not understand? Never say her name."

"Jesus Christ," I groan, flopping backward on my couch. "What was the revenge again? TP her house?"

"Egg it, but yeah. Toilet paper is actually quite fitting." She tries not to smile, waiting for us to inquire more about that connection. No one does. She finally gives up and explains it herself. "It's because she's a piece of shit!"

***

Finally giving in, we make our way to the gas station. It's the only place open at eleven p.m. At least, the only place open that sells eggs and toilet paper.

Otto is very reluctant. He hates her with every fiber of his soul, but he doesn't want us to do this because we pity him.

None of us pity him. We all hate her with everything in us as well.

Mine and Jessie's hatred takes on a different form from Roxanne's. She blindly hates her, hates how she hurt Otto. She thinks Gail is ridiculous and an awful person. All true.

Jessie and I hate her for somewhat of a different reason. It's personal for us. She didn't just insult Otto, she attacked his sickness. She doesn't even know what's going on. The problem is, when he would tell her things, she would ignore him. Everyone wants a word. A definition. People are always interested in the diagnoses. They don't say it out loud. People don't tend to ask you 'what do you have' as if you've got a common cold. They act weird about it, starting sentences they'll never finish. Wondering why you get 'special treatment' at school or why it's so hard for you to do normal things. They want to put you in a box and categorize you with the rest of the freaks. They want to know what exactly is wrong with your brain. I don't blame them, I wonder the same thing.

I've been diagnosed with two things. Social Anxiety Disorder and General Anxiety Disorder. When doctors or teachers ask, that's what I tell them. When people ask Jessie, they say General Anxiety and Depression. When people ask Otto, he says Anorexia Nervosa and Anxiety.

The thing is, those are just labels. They are words, they don't tell you anything at all. When someone hears anxiety, they think of scared little kids. When people hear social anxiety, they think of stutters and performance anxiety. People like Gail look at me funny when I talk about having suicidal ideation when I don't have Depression. They think, *don't you have anxiety? That isn't anxiety.* Anxiety is so much more than they think.

Labels don't tell the whole truth. They don't tell how stuff like that separates you from society. They don't tell you about the painful intrusive thoughts and time spent wishing you were different. You tell people you can't attend a class due to your anxiety, they think you're overreacting. 'Well everyone has anxiety', they say. I wish there was a way to prove it. I guess that's why thoughts always come, telling me to hurt or kill myself. Concrete proof I'm messed up. Concrete proof that I need help.

That's why it hurts so much when someone like Gail does something like that. Leaves you because your illness doesn't make sense to them. It tells you the truth. **Your**

sickness makes it impossible for anyone to have any sort of relationship with you.

That's why I need to do this to Gail. Why I need to let her know that what she did royally fucked us all up.

The dude working the till at the gas station stares at us with raised eyebrows. I guess it probably does look pretty crazy, four teenagers buying three cartons of eggs and a full case of toilet paper.

"Breakfast," I tell him. He just raises his eyebrows.

My friends crack up on the way out.

"What kind of breakfast are you having?" Otto guffaws.

".........eggs."

That statement inspires even more laughter.

Gail's house is close. Everyone's house is close, but hers is literally right beside the gas station. Like two buildings away.

"So how do we start this?" I ask in Roxanne's direction.

"Don't ask me, I'm just the ideas man."

"Wonderful."

"I guess we just start throwing them..?" Otto says cautiously. I take an egg out of the carton and toss it at the

129

house. It's the most ridiculous throw ever. It doesn't even hit the walls, it just falls to the dirt, making a slight splattering sound.

"That was pathetic," Roxanne laughs.

"Shut up. You try." I pass her an egg, which she promptly throws at the wall. It hits a slab of white trim, staining it a bright syrupy orange.

Jessie takes one and pelts it at a window. They freeze at a loud cracking sound.

"Welp, it was either the egg or the window," Otto says. "Doesn't affect us either way." He takes a roll of toilet paper and tosses it over a tree.

"Seriously?" I sigh. "This is supposed to be therapeutic for you. Throw shit at her house! She ruined your life!"

"She didn't ruin my life. I did that to myself."

"Fuck that!" Jessie shouts, placing an egg in Otto's palm. "Sorry. I didn't mean to talk so loudly," they apologize, covering their mouth with their hands.

Otto stares at the egg for a second. He runs his thumb over the smooth shell, a soft, thin skin over its dripping insides.

Just like so many of us.

He winds up like a pitcher, bringing out his inner baseball kid. He lets it fly with an earth-shattering holler, watching it soar through the darkness and landing right smack-dab on the front door. The rest of us whoop with cheers, tossing the rest of the eggs and toilet paper at the house.

Suddenly, the door swings open. A middle-aged man in a bathrobe pops out. Gail's dad.

"What the fuck are you doing kid?! Get out of here! I'm calling your mother!"

"Shit, shit, shit!" I hiss, tearing my friends away from the lawn. Roxanne seems pretty intent on staying, but the power of three people manages to pull her off the grass.

We take off in a run, laughing at the dad's incoherent insults.

"Where are we going?" Otto asks when we eventually slow to a walk.

"I dunno." Jessie shrugs. "But now we definitely can't go to Cecelia's house. He's going to call your mother!!!"

"Let's go to the beach. That was the most I've run since the third grade," I groan. "I'm sweating like a pig."

Chapter Seventeen

The water is as cool and comforting as it always is. I love reliable constants. Something that never changes. Something that is always good, or even always bad. I need to know how everything is going to go or I'll lose it.

"Truth or dare?" Roxanne suggests, her voice seeming as though it's coming from nowhere, given that the darkness has covered everyone's features.

"Sure. Who wants to go first?" I ask.

"I'll go," Otto decides. "Jessie, truth or dare?"

"Um... truth?" They say slowly. There are not many questions left to ask. We all kind of know everything about each other.

"Uh wait, I didn't actually have any ideas. Uh... what's your darkest secret?" he tries. We all instantly boo him.

"That question sucks! You have to actually ask a good one," I complain.

"Fine. What's... what's something embarrassing that no one knows about you?"

"Um... Oh. I have superhero bandaids. I insisted we get them. Does that count?" They grin.

"I mean, it's not embarrassing, it's incredible, but sure," I say "Your turn now."

"Okay." They swim in circles, trying to decide who to pick. "Cecelia, truth or dare."

"Truth."

"Do you think you'll ever get a life partner of any sort? I know you're aro-ace but I know some ace people consider their friends their 'soulmates' and live with them. What do ya think about that?"

Jessie's hilarious. Everyone else always asks truth questions like 'who do you like' or a 'smash or pass' kind of deal. Jessie goes into full-on dramatic philosophical questions.

"I don't know," I sigh, tipping backwards so I'm facing the starry sky. "I've thought of it. I consider all of you my soulmates of sorts. If Otto doesn't ever find anyone, he can for sure live with me. I have faith that you guys will stay together forever though," I tell Roxanne and Jessie.

"In another life, you and I would've been an insane power couple though bro." Otto chuckles.

"Oh for sure." I laugh. "Okay, my turn. Roxanne, truth or dare?"

"Dare. I actually have balls, unlike you all."

"Oh wow okay. Um... I dare you to retrieve something from the ground without using your hands!" I decide.

"What?" She recoils.

"I don't know, it was the first thing I thought of!"

She shakes her head but dives underwater for a good thirty seconds.

"Is she still alive?" Otto whispers. Just then, she resurfaces, a large rock between her teeth.

"That is disgusting, but impressive," I laugh.

"Whatever. Otto, truth or dare."

"Dare."

"I dare you to get a girlfriend," she says, entirely serious.

"What, right now?" He snorts.

"No, in university. I dare you to get a girlfriend who is kind and nice and amazing because you deserve it."

We all let that simmer for a while.

"...Damn," I say finally. "That was beautiful, Roxie."

Otto erupts into laughter, ripples casting out from where he's positioned in the water.

"Thanks, but no I don't deserve that."

"What are you talking about?!" Jessie gasps.

"Otto." I reach out under the waves and grab his shoulder. The cotton of his t-shirt is drenched all the way. It's only at this moment that I realize he's been shivering. I want to shield him, make him feel better. Make him see himself from my eyes. The hilarious person who can always make me feel better. "Don't fucking say that about yourself." I want to say more. I want to remind him of every time he passed me my earbuds when I got scared. Every panic attack he calmed me down from. How I might not be here today without him. Nobody talks about the insane difference your friends can have in your life. "Don't say that shit about my best friend."

He starts to chuckle a bit. "Yeah. Thanks, dude. Uh... Truth or dare?"

I hear that he's anxious to change the subject. You can't tell someone that hates themself that they are amazing. They won't believe you. I speak from experience. If someone compliments me, it's impossible for me to actually believe them. The little angry voices tell me the opposite.

Everyone hates you. Why did you say that? That was cheesy and ridiculous.

Ah, right on cue.

Ridiculous, predictable, anxious thoughts.

I hate them.

"Truth," I tell him.

"Booo!" Roxanne shouts. "You always pick truth! It's boring!"

This is true. Dares are terrifying. You never know what you're going to have to do. I don't want to risk it. I like knowing what's going to happen. I need to know what's going to happen. Truth is the safe, fun way of going about it. You don't need to risk your life, and you get to know the people you love better. It's a win-win.

"You have to pick 'dare' sometime, Cecelia!" Otto tells me. "That's the whole point of the game!"

"Dares are scary!"

"That's the point!" Roxanne and Otto shout at the same time.

"Fine. Dare." I say, giving in. I can tell that I'm not going to win this one.

"I dare you to... hold your breath as long as you can underwater," Otto decides.

"That's it? Okay." I inhale as much as I can before diving under the surface. My ears fill up until I can't hear anything anymore. I open my eyes, yet I can't see a thing. What if a shark came and ate me? Would I even notice until I was in immense pain? Are there sharks in lakes?

An overwhelming fear takes over every limb of my body. Not of the sharks, that's fine. I don't care about dying that much. It doesn't scare me. The thing that does scare me is the fact that I can't hear what my friends are saying right now.

They're talking about how much they hate you. They hope you drown under here. Why do you think they dared you to do this? They want you to die. Everyone would be better off if you died. You're going to lose them and life will have no point anymore. You'll lose them when you get to university. They are the only people who will ever somewhat like you. You are going to die alone.

The thoughts tumble over themselves and contradict each other. I see every possible bad scenario.

Die.

And for a moment, I consider it. Let go. Feel the water fill your lungs and keep you under.

Your friends are better off without you. They don't—

A hand grabs me by my shoulder and pulls me out from underwater. Jessie wraps their arms around me in a hug.

"That was a stupid dare, Cecelia, I'm sorry," Otto whispers.

"Please don't drown, mi amiga. We want you here," Jessie mumbles into my shoulder.

No, they don't.

But they wouldn't have saved me if they didn't want me here. Roxanne wouldn't have pulled me out of the water. Jessie wouldn't be hugging me. Otto wouldn't be so scared.

People want me here? I'm not just something they have to deal with?

I really fucking hope that's true.

I take a deep breath, thanking the universe that it's air filling my lungs instead of water.

"Do you guys wanna go home and watch a movie now?"

Chapter Eighteen

Twelfth Grade, January

It's time to go prom shopping. I have no idea what to get. I don't want to wear something pink or blue and 'be basic' but I also don't want to stand out too much. It's a very thin line to walk.

Roxanne and I have been talking about this for years. She's been set on the same idea since the sixth grade. She wants a deep red satin dress. One that swirls around her ankles and wraps over her shoulders. She has about a hundred pictures saved on her phone.

Otto and Jessie are coming along with us. Jessie said that they needed someone else's opinion, someone that isn't Otto. Otto doesn't care that much. When we asked him what he wanted to wear, he just said 'uh... a suit?'

We're all going as a group. It's too complicated for Roxanne and Jessie to go together, and Otto and I both don't have a partner. It'll be way more fun this way anyways.

Roxanne texts me, asking if I can drive her to the mall. We could walk, but there's so much snow right now it would be painful. I'm not too hyped about driving on frosty slippery roads, but it'll be fine.

I text back with a thumbs up and go out to my car. Even in thick corduroy pants, a huge sweater, and a humongous coat, I am still freezing. I can feel a chill in every one of my bones.

I started my car from inside my garage so it's nice and toasty when I get inside. I know it's awful for the environment but it's the only way to go in this part of Canada. If you don't pre-warm your car, it feels like you're stepping right into a giant freezer. Not that comfortable.

I never know what music to play in January. I play Christmas music for all of December, so when January comes I never have any playlists ready. I end up going with a list called 'Sleet'. It's a bunch of indie seventies songs about sad things. I named it Sleet because the songs give the same vibes as that weather. I don't really know how to describe it. A lot of my playlists are like that. Named after random things I associate with those songs. Sleet, cinnamon, sunscreen. I know, it's strange.

Roxanne comes running out to the car the second I pull up. A whiff of cold air sneaks in when she opens the door.

"Jesus, Cecelia. What is this depressing song?" She shivers as she sits down. It's actually one of my dad's favorite songs. Roxanne is not impressed. She picks up my phone and switches to my 'glitter' playlist. It's all my most girl boss songs. The tunes that make you want to break up with your partner for kicks and then rock a sparkly gown. It's one of Roxie's favorite playlists. Second only to 'dagger'. I feel like that one is pretty self-explanatory.

Roxanne starts singing loudly and painfully off-key. I roll my eyes as I turn into Jessie's driveway. Both them and Otto come out of the house looking positively freezing.

"Okay, y'all I'm kinda freaking out," Jessie announces as they slide into the backseat.

"What? Why?" I ask, glancing over my shoulder quickly to get an idea of their expression. They aren't in a full panic attack, which is good. They just kind of look like they're a little on edge.

"What do I wear to prom? Because I can't wear anything too.... gendered. But I don't want to wear something

boring and basic. I want to feel like... me. That sounds cheesy, I'm sorry."

"Nah you're good. What are you thinking?"

"I don't know! That's my problem right now!"

"So, probably not a dress or skirt or anything like that right?" I confirm.

"Yeah no, that doesn't seem like something I want to do right now." They shake their head.

"Okay, but you also don't want to wear a full tux?" Otto verifies.

"Have you considered... coming out to your parents?" Roxanne asks slowly. Everything in the car goes quiet except for the stereo screaming party songs. People don't really come out in Oublie. They tend to just stay in the closet until university when they maybe come out to their close friends. Internalized homophobia tends to take over. That's the case for literally everyone but Roxanne. She told everyone she was a lesbian the second she figured it out. Her parents are extraordinarily chill so she never had to worry about anything. They were only confused by why she was dating someone non-binary if she's gay, but Jessie has never really cared that Roxanne identifies as lesbian because Roxie considers a lesbian to be someone who 'isn't a dude that

doesn't like dudes'. She explained that to her parents and they were totally supportive.

Jessie's parents are a little different. They are incredibly religious. They've got Jesus quotes and crosses on their walls. Their parents are super nice people, but they say some questionable stuff sometimes. It's interesting to think about how they'd react to their kid coming out as a non-binary lesbian. I can't imagine that would go well.

"I don't know. I can't imagine telling them," they say quietly.

"Well, they know I'm gay." Roxanne shrugs. "They're pretty chill about it."

"Everyone knows you're gay, mi amor." Jessie rolls their eyes. "And I'm pretty sure they're in denial about it. They keep asking if you've finally got a boyfriend."

"EW!" she yells. "Men are gross. No offense, bro," she says in Otto's direction.

"None taken, men are gross," he agrees.

"Everyone is gross," I add.

"Women aren't gross," Otto and Roxanne say in unison.

"Guys, please stop saying the word gross." Jessie shakes their head as we pull into the mall parking lot. I brace myself for the cold as we run into a huge department store.

There aren't very many people in here today. Usually, there are a bunch, but I think there's some sort of outdoor hockey event going on, so everyone is there. That's why we decided to go shopping today.

Roxanne immediately dives into the racks, pulling out a bunch of dresses to try on. Otto stares at all the suits for a bit, before pulling out a nice deep blue one. He picks up a couple of other sizes for good measure.

Jessie and I stand in the middle of it all, unsure where to look first.

"I'll look for you, you look for me?" I suggest.

"Great plan." They run off into the dresses, clearly with an idea in mind. I don't really know where to start for their outfit though. That is until I see the vintage section. It's not necessarily prom stuff, but it's amazing. There are millions of old blouses and ridiculous floral-patterned suit jackets. After a bit of mixing and matching, I assemble the perfect outfit. It takes me a bit, but I finally find Jessie and present them with my selection.

Dijon coloured dress pants and coat. Feminine white blouse with puffed sleeves. And, the best part, an almost gold waistcoat. Vintage, androgynous, masterpiece.

Not to toot my own horn or anything, but I swear they look like they're about to tear up.

"Holy shit dude, that's perfect." They take the pieces from me and cradle them in their arms. "Oh, your dress is right there." They gesture towards a lilac gown sitting on one of the shelves.

It's the most beautiful dress I've ever seen.

Chapter Nineteen

Jessie has set up a campfire at the beach. They texted us to meet them there and to bring marshmallows. I'm a little nervous, it's not as late as it usually is when we go to the beach. It's only nine o'clock, so the sun is still setting. What if there are other people there? Will we get in trouble for lighting a fire? Will they think that we're ridiculous for eating s'mores?

That's only something little kids do. You have to be grown up now.

Breathe. No one will judge you. Everything is okay right now. You are safe.

I've noticed my mind getting a lot more concerned about my future lately. Not really like careers or anything, I'm pretty confident in that area. I have time. I'm terrified for the more personal side of my future. The mental illness side, one could say. I can't stop thinking about the worst-case scenario about what could happen to me. I could become addicted to my pills and end up on the street. I could get more illnesses, and end up crazy and alone. That's what the media shows you. Mental illness is scary. Mental illness ruins people's lives. Psychopathic murderers started out like you. Just. Like. You. It makes sense why some of us do end up like that. Because that's the expectation. Live up to the standards I guess.

I'm not saying I'm going to go on a killing rampage or anything. I'm just saying that I can understand why some people do.

You sound insane.

Yeah, that's my point. I don't know.

I need to go to the beach.

My campfire outfit consists of jean shorts, a bikini top, and a short-sleeve plaid overshirt.

You look ridiculous. Trying too hard. Ugly. Fake. Ridic–

OKAY. Shake my head. Reset the thoughts. Stop it, stop it, stop it. I look great. I look awesome. I look super cool.

Besides, even if I don't, it doesn't really matter. The only people that'll be there are my friends. Maybe some randos, but there's barely any sunlight left. No one will be able to see me.

Those are the words I repeat to myself on my way to the beach. I meet Otto at the T intersection between our houses.

"Did Jessie's text seem more... urgent than usual?" he asks.

Now that I think about it, there was a period in their text. They never use periods. I overlooked it because their tone didn't seem too mad. Is something wrong? Are they mad? Why would they be mad? Did I do something to upset them? Every single thing I've done in the past week runs through my head. What did I do?

"Crap, Cecelia. I didn't mean to scare you. I'm sure everything's fine." He squeezes my shoulder to comfort me.

"Did I do something?" I ask.

"Not that I know." He shrugs. "Besides, Jessie never gets mad about anything. The longest they've been mad at me was like two days."

"Okay. That's good."

The beach approaches faster than I was ready for. I can see the light from the flames illuminating the trees. I can't help but imagine the whole forest becoming engulfed in smoke. I can practically hear the crackling burning of the trees.

Nope. Not right now.

Jessie and Roxanne have dragged some large rocks and stumps to make some form of chairs around the pit.

"Hey!" Jessie says, waving us over. They don't sound mad at all. Yet, a part of my brain keeps yelling at me about it. **You shouldn't have said that thing. You shouldn't have done that thing.**

"What's going on? What's with the scary urgent message?" I ask.

"What? No, not scary." They shake their head. "I just have some news. Or, plans. Soon-to-be news."

"Hon, you're rambling," Roxanne tells them.

"Right. Um... I have decided what the next item on the bucket list should be."

Otto and I share a glance of confusion. All this for the bucket list?

"What is it?" Otto implores.

"Um... I might– I'm gonna come out to my parents." Their words drift out without a reply. No one knows what to say.

"...Are you sure?" Otto says dubiously.

"Otto!" I hiss.

"What? I'm just saying... I know Tia Tiffany and I know Tio Bruno. I don't... I don't know how good of an idea this is. Couldn't it wait until you go to university?"

"I've thought of this quite a bit, Otto," Jessie tells him firmly. "It's the best thing. If they can't accept it, Roxie said I could live with her until autumn. I've been saving up emergency money since I was fourteen. It'll be okay." Their voice shakes a bit, but I can tell they've made up their mind. This is going to happen.

"So, what can we do to help?" I ask.

"I don't know," they sigh.

"Okay."

"How are you going to tell them?" Otto wonders. "We'll be there for you if you need us."

"Yeah," I agree. "We could even come in with you if you want that. Whatever you need."

"I think it's best if I do it alone." They sigh. "They'll think you guys brainwashed me or something. I'm just so scared that they're going to kick me out." A tear slides down their cheek as they think about it. "How would I live with myself?"

"Look at me." I take them by the arm. "You are not your parents' opinions. You are so much more than that."

They nod but their shoulders continue to shake with sobs.

"Hey, it's okay," Roxie soothes. I've never seen her so comforting. That's usually Jessie's role. "Do you want to change the subject?"

They nod their head vigorously. "Someone else talk."

"I ate a donut today!" Otto says quickly. "Sorry, that was stupid, I was just trying to think of something."

"Otto!" I yell. "That is not stupid! That's incredible! How are you doing? Was it delicious? What kind? I love donuts."

"Clearly," he laughs, " I am doing okay. I wasn't doing well for a bit but now I feel okay. It was so tasty bro. I forgot how amazing donuts are. It was jam-filled."

I'm kinda surprised that he remembered all of my many questions.

Jessie stands up to give Otto a hug. They whisper something in his ear which makes him smile. He replies with a simple "That's what she said."

"What?! Now I want to know what the joke was!" Roxanne exclaims. Otto sticks his tongue out at her.

"My anxious thoughts have gotten a lot worse lately," I tell them.

Example A: **Why did you say that? You ruined the vibe. Everyone hates you.**

"I feel you with that one," Jessie groans. "My intrusives have been going crazy. Yesterday I almost took a bite of my bar of soap and then I almost took a bite of my arm. It was a crazy shower." We all laugh a little at Jessie's unhinged thoughts, but something in them rings a little too true.

"I'm scared," I whisper. "What if I hurt myself again, but I'm at university so I'm alone? What happens then?"

"You text your therapist?" Roxanne offers.

Something tells me that that won't do much. I've only hurt myself once before, and it wasn't really on purpose. My intrusive thoughts told me that I should shave the hair on my back. Don't do that. I shaved the skin off, but I kept going. I had weird scrape marks on my back for a couple of weeks, but they went away eventually. It was terrifying, but I called Jessie immediately after and we all went out for ice cream to take my mind off it. What if that happens at university? When I have no one to distract me?

What happens then?

"Yeah, she's really busy. Sometimes we have to do our appointments over a video call."

"That's kinda weird, I didn't know people did that," she muses.

I roll my eyes at Roxanne's obliviousness. I find it easier to talk to my therapist over a call. I'm in my own room, my own safe space. I like it better that way.

Chapter Twenty

I wake up Monday morning to a text from Jessie in all caps. It was sent at four a.m. this morning.

'I'M READY'.

What?

Forgetting the fact that I just woke up and look terribly awful, I start a video call with the whole group. Otto answers right away, and Jessie picks up seconds later. Roxanne is in the frame with them. Their background is all trees.

"Where are you guys?" I ask.

"The forest," Roxanne informs us.

"Okay... Jessie, what are you ready for?" I question.

"Oh yeah. I'm ready to tell my parents. We planned a lot yesterday, and I think I'm ready."

"Seriously?" Otto gapes.

I don't know their family that well. Otto's parents are really nice, and their dads are brothers, but I guess siblings turn out differently sometimes. I've only had like, two conversations with Jessie's parents, and they seemed pretty chill, but that might just be because I can come off as a mentally stable straight girl to a lot of people. It's a sad truth.

"Can you guys come with me?" Jessie asks.

"Like... to come out to your parents? I don't think we're supposed to be there for that." I say.

"No, not to come inside or anything, but could you meet us here and then walk me there? Stay outside until I'm done? I want you all to be the first people to know how it goes." They've clearly thought this all out quite a bit. The plan doesn't make a ton of sense to me, but it's okay. I just have to go meet Jessie and Roxanne in the forest and then figure it out from there. I'm sure Roxanne has a much better understanding of the plan than I do right now.

***

"Jessie." Otto stares into their eyes. "Are you sure you're ready to do this?"

Otto's always taken a sort of older brother position for Jessie. He's only two months older, and Jessie is a lot taller than him, so it's a bit of a funny dynamic, but it's understandable. He's known them their whole life, he's been there for everything. He understands them in a way nobody else ever could.

"Yeah. I am." Jessie says.

"Okay."

"Okay." The cousins smile at each other, sharing a moment that the rest of us will never understand.

"Let's do this thing!" Roxanne yells, changing the vibe a little bit. I let out a loud whoop and start to play my 'confetti' playlist. It's mostly just eighties disco music with a couple of overplayed early 2000s pop songs.

I keep forgetting how bloody hot it is outside. I can feel the heat from the cement through my sandals. Climate change is really taking its toll on our town. I think it's closer to forty degrees Celsius than it is to thirty. Insane.

Even though the air is barely breathable, I break out into a sort of skip, dancing around.

You look ridiculous.

It doesn't matter. I'm just trying to take Jessie's mind off of what they're about to do.

"We should go to the beach after," I tell them.

"Yeah," Jessie mumbles. Clearly, my distraction methods aren't working that well.

"I'm not sure that we'll be in the swimming mood after this." Roxanne sighs.

Right.

Stupid. That was a selfish thing to say. Everyone hates you.

I close my eyes and tilt my head up so the sun hits my face. Breathe. The sun feels nice.

It's burning your eyelids. You're gonna get skin cancer. You're gonna die.

Good.

Breathe. The sun feels nice. Inhale, two, three, four. Hold, two, three, four. Exhale, two, three, four, five, six. Hold, two, three, four.

A hand settles on my shoulder, making me jump slightly. I open my eyes to see Jessie looking at me, their eyebrows raised with concern.

"It's okay," they tell me.

This is wrong. This is all wrong. They shouldn't be worried about me, I should be worried about them. Why do I do this? **Why do I make everything about me?**

"I'm sorry," I whisper.

"You have nothing to be sorry for. You can't control it."

I can't control it.

"It's not your fault."

It's not my fault.

"Thank you," I whisper.

"We should go to the beach after. That would be nice."

A sickly feeling settles in my gut. The self-loathing is debilitating. **You're faking it. You're just trying to get people to feel bad for you. They're going through a crisis and you're making it all about you. Selfish.**

But I can't stay in a thought loop like this. I can't keep overthinking everything, or I'll never stop. I'll stay in the cycle forever. I can't do that, because today is Jessie's day. Today, I need to be there for them.

Everyone stops suddenly. I look up, stumbling slightly when I realize we've reached Jessie's house.

"Are you ready?" Roxanne asks. They shake their head, but start to walk up to the doorway nevertheless.

"We'll be here," I promise. "We'll be here the whole time."

They nod but don't look back, just open the door and step in.

"So..." Otto starts. "How are we feeling?"

"I'm terrified," Roxanne announces. She twiddles her hair between two of her fingers. The same piece of hair she twirls when she's flirting. This is a first. Roxanne doesn't tend to get scared. She's the rock, the always confident, fearless one. "What if they react really badly? What if they hurt them? What if they send them away?" I hear the panic in her voice. It's something I've never heard from her before. It's a bit of a shock, realizing your heroes are scared too. It's embarrassing to call her my hero, but it's true.

"It'll be okay," I tell her, having no evidence to back up that statement. "They'll be eighteen in October. They'll be able to leave their parents if it's bad." I have to keep repeating this over and over. They can leave if it's bad. They won't be stuck somewhere awful. They could stay with Roxanne. It might be bad at first. God knows they've experienced enough bad things for a lifetime. People that sweet aren't supposed to have to deal with stuff that awful.

What if they hurt them and I didn't do anything to protect them? What if it's my fault?

I want to tell them that their parents don't define who they are. The words their parents say won't define who they are for the rest of their life. They need to know that. Should I do something? It's been a while, what is happening?

I lie down on the grass and close my eyes. I can't keep spiraling in these thoughts. Breathe.

The sun envelops me like a blanket. You wouldn't think that the smell of sunscreen and sweat would be a good smell, but somehow it is. Somehow, it is one of the best smells ever.

Distraction methods work for long enough. Long enough for Jessie to come running out of the house. They don't look hurt. Physically, at least. There are tears running down their face, but a sly smile on their face.

"It's okay!" they shout, flopping down beside me. "It's okay. They didn't kick me out. They just... They said it was a phase, but that's one of the best-case scenarios. They also said Jesus would be disappointed, that he only created two sexes for a reason. It doesn't matter, I don't care about Jesus that much," they sigh and continue to mumble their thoughts. "I know they're going to keep calling me by the wrong pronouns, but better than living on the street, I guess." Their voice cracks a bit on the last words.

Roxanne wraps them into a hug, whispering comforting words in their ear. "I'm so proud of you."

"I argued with them about it, but they weren't budging," they mumble. "It's okay. It doesn't matter, because it's not a phase. I know that, you know that, and I'm pretty sure Jesus knows that! They'll realize it eventually. Until then, who wants to go to the beach?"

Chapter Twenty-One

Twelfth Grade, June

It's prom night. I can't believe it's finally prom night.

I'm not ready. What if I freak out? What if I have a panic attack in the middle of the dance floor and ruin the night for everyone?

I haven't been able to bring myself to put my dress on yet. I had a brief freak-out because I couldn't figure out what bra to wear, so I've been trying not to think about getting dressed.

I've been stuck in the same spot for the last twenty minutes. I'm in a fetal position on my bed, my phone sitting on my knees. I feel the most safe here, in this position. I could stay here for hours watching mind-numbing videos on my phone. It's probably not a very healthy coping mechanism, but it gets the job done. Or, delays it at least.

A text pops up from Roxanne, interrupting my video. Attachment: 1 image. It's a photo of her in her dress. She looks amazing. It's blood red and satin, just like she always wanted. It's fitted around her torso and hips but it flares out on her legs. It's beautiful.

I text her back some heart-eye emojis, feeling dread in my stomach for the inevitable question coming next.

'Thanks! Can u send a pic of urs?'

Nope. No, I can't. Because it's still in my closet and I'm on my bed. Those three steps to the closet are far more than I am able to do right now.

'I'm not dressed yet.'

She replies with a lot of capital letters and a lot of curse words. Now she's coming over. Damn it. I think the door downstairs is open. I won't have to go unlock it.

It's ridiculous that that's my main concern right now, but I'll probably be able to get up when she's here. I hope I will.

"CECELIA!!!" I could hear her shouts from a mile away. She sounds angry at first, but her tone changes when she sees me. "Are you okay?"

"I don't know. I can't get out of bed. I don't know what to do."

"Okay. I know what you need to do. Get dressed. That's your first step."

"I don't know what bra to wear," I say quietly. It's ridiculous. I sound like an eleven-year-old.

"You don't need to wear a bra." She snorts. "Most dresses have built-in padding. It'll be fine."

Oh. Okay.

She goes into my closet and retrieves the dress. "This is going to be the best night ever. You can't let anxiety ruin it for you."

Maybe I should be insulted by that. Maybe I should be mad at her. But everything she's saying sounds pretty reasonable.

"Okay," I whisper. I fling my legs over the side of my bed so I'm sitting up.

"I'll go wait right outside. Shout when you're done." She leaves, closing the door behind her. Since I'm sitting up, I can probably get up. Every part of my body feels like it's being weighed down by a thousand bricks, but I stand up nevertheless.

The old tee shirt and boxer shorts go off. The dress goes on. It's a weird transition, going from dirty pajamas to a sparkling gown. I wait until the very last second to look at myself in the mirror. I don't want my mind to be mean.

When I'm done, it is time to look. It's time to see if I look good.

Turn to the mirror.

Oh.

You look amazing.

That's a new kind of thought. My strong thoughts aren't typically hyping me up, but it's kinda true. I do look amazing.

It's the most beautiful lavender color and the bodice is covered in floral lace designs. It's gorgeous. I feel gorgeous.

"You can come in," I say quietly.

Roxanne flings the door open and brings her hands to her mouth.

"Girl. You are stunning. Holy shit." She gasps. "Can I do your hair?"

"Yeah of course." I wasn't going to do it; I literally have no concept of how to do formal hairstyles.

She makes me sit down on the ground and gets to work braiding my hair. She keeps my signature hairstyle, two braids,

165

but she makes them look fancy. Instead of plain braids that hang down by my ears like ropes, she does Dutch braids with flowers woven in. I guess she brought them for this occasion, with this hairstyle in mind.

"Roxanne, this is too much."

"It's perfect. Now we have to do your makeup." She reaches for my concealer when her phone starts ringing.

"Hello?" she answers. There are muffled sounds coming from the other end that I can't understand.

"Okay, we're basically ready." She hangs up and looks at me. "We've gotta go."

"But... my makeup?"

You look ugly without makeup. You need to keep your face covered. You have an ugly zit on your forehead, everyone will notice. You'll be that girl that looked disgusting at prom.

"You don't need it. You're already glowing."

Oh damn.

"Maybe you're pregnant."

Never mind, she ruined it. There's a knock at the door downstairs. Is that for us?

"Time to go!" She throws my phone, wallet, keys, and a book into a tote bag. She knows me so well. The bag brings a little more of me into the outfit. It's perfect.

We walk down the stairs in a dramatic princess-style greeting. By that point, Otto and Jessie have let themselves in. They look amazing. Jessie's smile could light up a city, especially when they see Roxanne.

Otto starts cheering when he sees us.

"I can't believe I'm friends with girls that are this gorgeous and I don't have a chance with either of them. What is the universe trying to tell me?" he laments.

"It's trying to tell you that you'll have no bitches for the rest of your life." I grin.

He recoils, bringing his hand to his heart. "You wound me."

"Sorry bro." I swing my arm around his shoulder and we make our way outside, leaving Roxanne and Jessie to do whatever lovebird stuff they need to do inside.

It's pouring rain. It's the hot June rain, the kind that makes your clothes stick to your back. I use my bag as a temporary umbrella, praying that my book doesn't get wet in the distance from my house to the car.

Otto's parents lent us their car. I'm driving because I'm always the driver. Just like I always host our sleepovers. Shit, am I the mom friend?

Otto slides into the passenger's seat and I take my place behind the wheel. I love Otto's car, everything from the chipped paint to the initials scratched into the leather of the seat. JD and OD. Jessie and Otto Diaz.

I hope this car stays around forever. Otto's car is way nicer than my car. Where his has shiny black leather seats, mine's got mysteriously stained fabric gray ones. His smells like coffee and mint, and mine smells like old tea and fries. Everything about the Diaz's car is prettier, fancier, and classier than mine. It makes sense why we chose this one to drive to the prom. It's iconic.

Otto connects his phone to the aux and plays his sports hype songs. I'm not sure that's the vibe for prom night, but okay.

Roxanne and Jessie hop into the backseat, hands intertwined.

"Are y'all ready to do this thing?!" Roxanne hoots. The car erupts in shouts. The rain pelts the windshield as I pull out onto the street.

Let's do this thing.

Chapter Twenty-Two

"Okay, we only have a couple of items left on the bucket list," I say as we're watching our regular Friday night movie. "What should we do next?"

"I have an idea," Roxanne announces. "I propose that we get tattoos." She says it so nonchalantly as if it isn't something that will permanently be on our skin forever. No biggie.

"Are we actually going to do that?" Jessie gapes. "I thought it was a joke! What would we even get?"

"I thought we should get something that would remind us of this summer. Something that will always make us remember this." Roxanne pulls out her phone and starts to show us photos.

"But... what if something happens? Won't we regret it?" I worry.

"What would happen?" Otto asks.

"Like, one of us becomes an ax murderer or something. Isn't it too risky?" I know that most of my fears are irrational. You don't have to tell me. Many therapists already have.

"I don't see that happening." Roxanne laughs.

"Okay but like, what if one of us dies and then we can't look at our body without feeling sad?" I say. Am I just trying to think of excuses? Maybe. Is that bad? No.

The three of them share a look like they all know something I don't. I hate that look. It's too middle school-y. It's mean.

"Hello?!" I yell, making them jump a little bit. "What's that look about?!"

"Wouldn't it be kinda nice though?" Jessie wonders. "A permanent reminder of the friendship. Kinda cool."

"What, you're on board now?!" I demand.

"It sounds kinda dope. You have to admit."

It kinda does. A reminder of this summer, of this friendship. Of a part of me I will never lose. About what these people mean to me.

Why won't you do it? You're ruining the whole thing for your friends.

"Fine. What should we get?"

"I like this one," Jessie says, pointing to an image on Roxanne's phone. It's a lineart of a sunrise over water. I've gotta admit, it's really pretty. I could get on board with that.

"That's awesome," Otto mutters.

"Let's do it!!" Roxanne shouts.

An angry swarm of moths forms in my chest. It's like butterflies in your stomach, but twelve times worse. You want to throw up, pass out, and cry at the same time. It happens to me at least three times per day.

Right now, it's a little different. The angry moths and the excited butterflies have morphed into one species all over my body. It feels terrible and incredible at the same time.

You sound insane.

"Okay fine, let's get it."

We pile into my car and everyone starts yelling addresses for me to write into the GPS.

"Okay! Quiet." I demand. "What's the closest one?"

Apparently, the closest tattoo parlor is sixty kilometers away. Road trip! Sunscreen playlist goes on, hats go off. I roll down all the windows so Otto can stick his head out the window like a dog. If you try hard enough, it is possible to romanticize rural Canadian highways.

We make a game of calling out every animal we see.

"Goat!"

"Horse!"

"Deer!"

It entertains us for a good ten minutes, and by the time we get bored, we're already in the city. None of us are used to navigating city streets so we end up going around the same block at least four times.

"Is that it?" Jessie asks, pointing to a sketchy hole-in-the-wall tattoo parlor.

"I guess so." I parallel park and step out of the car. City air smells so much different than small-town air. It smells like cars and rain, even in the middle of summer. The countryside smells like shit and wheat. People need to stop using animal manure on their farms, it's disgusting.

The tattoo parlour is the grungiest place I've ever seen. There are two faded pleather couches and a single chair in the middle surrounded by equipment. In the back, there's a single curtain. It must lead to the rest of the chairs. I hope everything here has been sanitized well. I've heard that if tattoo equipment isn't sanitized properly you can get STIs.

A bald middle-aged lady wearing a bandana and braids comes out from behind the curtain. She's covered in tattoos of a bunch of different flowers, one of which is a rose that wraps around her neck and blooms on the back of her head.

"Hey. You have an appointment?" she asks me.

"Uh... no." I glance at my friends, who shrug. "Do you do walk-ins?"

"Yeah, just wanted to make sure. You're over eighteen?" she asks.

I nod.

"Okay great. Sit down there."

I'm kinda surprised she didn't ask for ID. **RED FLAG RED FLAG!!!! This place is illegal. You're going to get seriously infected. You'll lose your arm. You'll never be able to write again.**

"We're gonna go back there to get our tattoos," Otto says, gesturing towards the curtain on the back wall.

"Wait!" I exclaim, my voice cracking. "Don't leave me, I can't do this alone."

"It's okay, you're going to have to do stuff like this by yourself when we're gone. Think of it like practice." Otto smiles and the three of them disappear behind the curtain, leaving only me, the tattoo lady, and a bunch of needles. That's not scary at all. **You're going to die.**

"What would you like?" the tattoo lady asks, whose name tag, I'm now realizing, says 'Gertie'. I show her the photo of the sun, explaining the spot on my wrist where I'd like it.

She starts to disinfect the area and prepares her equipment.

"Do you sanitize the needles?" I ask without thinking.

"What?" She raises her eyebrows.

"I just... the lady that gave us the sex talk in eighth grade said you could get HIV from tattoo equipment." My words spill over each other, announcing to this poor woman how crazy I truly am.

"I promise, we sanitize them after every customer." She smiles. "Also, we barely ever get anyone in here, so there's nothing to be worried about."

Huh. That's reassuring I guess. She starts to draw the design out with a pen. That's when I close my eyes and try not to think about what's about to happen.

I can't believe I'm doing this. I can't believe I'm getting a tattoo.

You're going to become addicted to the pain and use it as a form of self-harm.

Jesus! I almost jerk in my seat from that thought, making me open my eyes, and that's when I see the needle. It's thicker than I expected. I thought it would look like a syringe or a sewing needle. But it's bigger and sharper and heading towards my arm and I'm going to die and I'm going to lose my arm and I'm going to get addicted and—

It hurts. It really hurts. But it's not the worst pain I've ever felt. It feels hot, like a fresh bee sting. Except, the stinger is being dragged along my skin.

Still, it hurt more when I broke my arm in the fifth grade.

"What's your name, hun?" Gertie asks.

"Uh, Cecelia." My eyes are focused on the needle and my skin and the needle and the ink and my skin and—

"That's a nice name. Can you take a deep breath for me, Cecelia?"

"Uh, yeah." I close my eyes and inhale, feeling my diaphragm expand and deflate. The same action I've done with a million therapists, counselors, teachers, and parents. This is my first tattoo artist though.

Before I know it, I'm done. And I love it. It looks so cool. All four of them look so cool. The second we leave the parlor, we take a photo of the four of our bandaged arms. I post it with the caption 'all tatted up'. I instantly get a bunch of likes and some comments saying they're 'glad to see me doing well'. I didn't know I was that obviously mentally ill.

"I can't believe we actually just did that," Jessie exclaims on the car ride home. "My parents are going to kill me! First the whole trans/gay thing and now this?! The bible literally said 'You shall not make gashes in your flesh for the dead, or incise any marks on yourselves.'"

"Bro, do you have the whole bible memorized?" Otto laughs.

"Not all of it. Just the parts about what I'm not supposed to do."

I bite my tongue to stop myself from saying 'isn't that all of it?' Jessie has a complicated relationship with religion, so I try my best not to make fun of it.

"They don't need to know. Just wear long sleeves around them for the next month, I bet they won't even notice," Roxanne offers.

"Yeah, yeah, okay."

The rest of the drive is spent discussing our tattoos and how we're now cooler than everyone else our age. Before we know it, we're back in Oublie.

"Are we hanging out tomorrow?" I ask once we're out of the car before everyone heads to their own houses.

"I don't know," Jessie says slowly, looking at Roxanne.

"I don't think so." Roxie shakes her head. "I think you're okay now."

"What?" I mutter, confused. "What do you mean?"

"You can do this now, Cecelia. You're going to be okay on your own." Otto smiles. "Bye. I love you."

"...Bye."

"I love you, Cecelia," Roxanne smirks and walks away.

"Love you." Jessie gives me a quick hug before running to catch up with Roxanne.

"Love you..." I murmur, confused.

"You'll be okay," Otto repeats, turning to walk away.

What do they mean? Are they leaving? **They've hated you this entire time. They were just your friends because they pitied you. They're going to stop being your friends now that you're stable. You should hurt yourself to prove you still need them.**

"Stop it!" I yell out loud.

They're just being weird. It's a prank. We'll hang out again tomorrow and everything will be normal.

Chapter Twenty-Three

Sunday morning is a perfect morning. Sun shining, birds tweeting, all the usual stuff. I lie in bed watching sitcoms for a while, smiling and laughing to myself. I've forgotten all about our weird conversation last night, and our even weirder conversation that we had over text.

I read over the messages from last night as I'm going to ask them to hang out. I can't seem to decode what Roxanne was saying.

'The last thing on the list is going to a funeral.'

I replied with 'We don't know anyone who has died'.

She then said 'Yes we do.'

Immediately after, Jessie texted. 'Stop, mi amor. Don't do it like this.' After that, nobody said anything else. I tried to ask about it, but there was no reply.

Just like last night, no one replies to my invite, so I decide to just swing by their houses and see if they want to go swimming.

I get dressed in my swimsuit and shorts and make my way downstairs, spraying myself with sunscreen as I go.

Both my parents are sitting on the kitchen island, talking in hushed voices.

"She seems okay," my mom whispers.

"It doesn't make sense, something is up," my dad replies.

"Hey guys," I say, announcing myself to the room.

"Hi! Are you headed to the beach?" Dad asks.

"Yeah, I'm just gonna go and get the others first," I tell them.

"What... what others?" My mom stutters.

"You know, my friends? Jessie, Otto, and Roxanne? I literally don't know anyone else." I shake my head and walk outside. My parents stay sitting at the island, stunned expressions on their faces. I don't know what's going on with them.

I walk to Roxanne's house first, a spring in my step. Little kids pass by, giggling and spraying each other with water guns. I hate it, but my thoughts envision a car coming by and taking them all out. Jesus Christ. I didn't need to see that.

I close my eyes, shake my head, and look at them again. Three of them, all alive and safe. What is wrong with my brain?

Everything.

I love Roxanne's house. I spent almost all of my childhood here. I could walk the route in my sleep. The house itself is a beige color, but the door is bright red. The curtains to the living room are closed, which is kinda weird. They're always open. Even at ten o'clock at night, you can see whatever royal drama her parents are watching that night.

I knock on the door with a gold doorknocker Roxanne insisted they get when she was little. I hear a soft patter of footsteps coming down the stairs, the lock clicking quietly.

Mrs. Devi opens the door. I love the woman, and I could never say anything bad about her, but she looks awful. She's wearing her signature red bathrobe and slippers, but that's when the resemblance to her old self stops. Her hair is a graying tangled mess. She usually dyes the roots, but I guess she hasn't in a while. Her usually vibrant makeup is gone, replaced with dark circles and sagging cheeks. She looks tired.

"...Mrs. Devi?"

"Cecelia." She smiles and inhales, her breath shaky. "Would you like to come in?"

I want to ask more about what's going on with her. I hope everything with her and Mr. Devi is okay.

"Ah, that's okay." I sigh. "I was just wondering if Roxanne wanted to go to the beach?"

"Roxanne?" Her face falls. Did she think I was there to see her? That's sort of strange. "She's gone."

"Oh really? Did she already go to the beach? Are the others with her?" I ask.

"Cecelia, are you okay?" Her eyes are as wide as saucers. I'm sick of people asking me that. They were probably going to text me, asking me to come. It was probably a mistake. I should be with them.

"Yeah, I'm fine. I'll go look at the beach, thanks. See ya!" I run down the stairs and to the beach.

They didn't invite you on purpose. They hate you. Why would you go and ruin the fun?

I don't care. I go to the beach anyway. It's filled to the brim with people. Everyone I know. Everyone except for them. Where are they?

Maybe Roxanne went somewhere with her band friends or something. Maybe the others aren't even with her. I'll check their houses.

As I'm walking away, I see Mrs. Devi peeking her head out the curtained window. She's on the phone with someone. Weird. I hope she's okay. I'll ask Roxanne later what's going on with her.

Nobody answers at Otto's house. I hear his dog barking inside and when I look up, I can see his little brother Milo's face in the window. On a nice summer day, a fourteen-year-old boy should be hanging out with his friends. Although I guess that he could be playing video games. I didn't think he was that nerdy, but people can surprise you.

Otto's clearly not here. The last house that I check is Jessie's. I'm kinda dreading it, their parents are pretty scary. I know they like me, from the outside I look like a kiss-ass, rule-abiding virgin, which I guess is true. People's parents love me. Best influence on the block. Kids hate it, but adults love it. That'll go well for me in the future, I hope. It's how I've gotten all my best grades in the past.

I walk slowly to Jessie's, rehearsing my lines in my head. I know that it's not that big of a deal, that I've talked to these people a billion times before. It's fine.

Breathe.

Instead of going straight there, I take a detour to Muriels. I have a sinking feeling that something is wrong, that my friends are doing something I don't want to know about. They're hanging out without me, talking about how much they hate me. They're dead on the side of the road, murdered overnight. They're doing drugs, laughing about how I'm too much of a goody-two-shoes to do it with them.

My therapist says that my imagination is my superpower. It's my greatest strength and my greatest weakness.

I can craft intricate stories and made-up worlds, but I can also convince myself that everyone hates me.

It sucks. I want a new superpower.

I know plenty of people with no creativity that are perfectly happy.

I buy a popsicle and a bag of chips from Muriel. Then it's time to go figure out what is happening with my friends. Where they are.

Walk the path I've walked before. Count the steps in each square of the sidewalk. One two, one two, one two three.

One two, one two, one two three.

There's a pretty flower on the side of the road, so I pull out my phone to take a picture. I have six missed calls from my mom, four from my dad, and one from Mrs. Devi. I'll call them back after I find Jessie.

I was at Jessie's house just days ago, when they came out to their parents. That feels like forever ago now, but the house hasn't changed one bit.

I ring the doorbell, listening to the clattering of high heels inside. Mrs. Diaz opens the door, appearing a bit shocked when she sees me. She's dressed from head to toe in black, the only exception being the silver cross that hangs over her chest. She's wearing a formal dress, the kind you'd wear to a funeral. Is she going to a funeral? I thought I'd know. Is that where Otto's family is? Is that why Mrs. Devi was so upset? Is that what Roxanne was talking about last night?

"Cecelia." Mrs. Diaz looks me up and down, taking in my bathing suit and sunglasses. "Are you not going to the service?"

"What service?" I ask. "I just wanted to see if Jessie or maybe Otto or Roxanne wanted to hang out, but I can't find any of them."

"Cecelia." She gasps, bringing her hands to her mouth. It takes everything in her to choke out her next couple of words. "Jessie... Otto... Honey, they're all dead."

Chapter Twenty-Four

Twelfth Grade, June

Happy car ride home from the prom. Listening to chill music, laughing at Roxanne's sloppy drunkness. Rainy roads, blurry street lights. My hands were on the wheel, eyes drifting shut on the road. A car coming out of nowhere. Their screams. What–

***

Flashing lights, blue and red. Siren sounds aching in my ears. Every part of me is warm and hurting. I'm on fire. What's going on?

Hands on my shoulder, picking me up and putting me on a stretcher. People around me, pumping air into my lungs. Where's Otto?

I can't see anything, only blurry lights and the moon through the window. Someone is talking to me, whispering comforting phrases. I don't understand, where am I?

Panic rushes through me like blood in my veins. I can't breathe. Where am I? What's going on? The confusion is too much. I wave my arms around, trying to shove everyone away from me. I want to go home. I don't want to be here anymore. I want it to be Friday night again. I want to watch movies with my friends in my basement again. I don't want to be here. Something sharp goes into my arm. Ow–

***

Hospital doors. E.R. Mrs. Devi? The smell of nighttime air hits differently.

***

Blackout.

***

Eyes open. White bed sheets, blue gown. Wet cheeks, cold nose. A quiet, calm beep. Beep. Beep.

I'm in a hospital. There's a tube in my arm. It's uncomfortable, I want it gone. I don't want to be here anymore.

My parents are in chairs beside my bed. My dad has his head in his hands and my mom is staring at the ceiling. I try to speak to them, but when I open my mouth, no sound comes out. I need water. I'm so thirsty.

I raise my hand slightly, pain shooting through my arm as I do. My mom's head snaps down until she's staring me right in the eye.

"Cecelia?" she whispers, her eyes filling with tears. My mom never cries. My dad looks up at me, his palms over his mouth.

"...Mom." Even one word hurts. A nurse rushes into the room, a clipboard in his hand.

"Hey, Cecelia," he says. "Would you like some water?"

I nod my head rapidly despite the blistering headache I have. He fills a cup and passes it to me. The water is lukewarm and tastes slightly like eggs, but it's the best thing I've ever had in my entire life.

"What happened?" I ask when I've regained my voice.

"Cecelia." Mom's voice cracks. It's too much. Whatever happened was too much. She breaks down in sobs, clutching her torso.

"You had surgery. There was an accident," my dad mumbles, wrapping an arm around my Mom. The nurse takes over for them, opening the door so they can leave. I'm sort of hurt that they did, but whatever happened must've been too horrible for them to talk about. Usually, I'd be thinking up a million scenarios. What might've happened. Today I can't. My brain is too tired, too hurt, or possibly too drugged to imagine anything.

Usually, I'd be worried about being left alone in a room with a stranger. Today, the thought barely crosses my mind.

"Cecelia. What is the last thing you remember?" he asks.

"Um... leaving the prom. What happened?"

"Okay. It was really rainy when you left the prom. There was a car on the road that lost control. It hit your car—"

"It's not my car. It's my friend Otto's dad's car," I interrupt. I don't know why that was an important detail to add. Maybe they should know for insurance or something.

"Otto, was he with you in the car?"

"Yeah, Otto, Roxanne, and Jessie. They were with me. Are they here? Did they need surgery too?" I look him in the eye, begging for answers.

"Okay. I'm really sorry to tell you this, Cecelia, but they didn't make it."

The rest of his words don't matter. The explanation, the apology. They don't matter. What matters is the fact that they're gone. The three people I love most in the world. The only people that were ever there for me. The only people that ever truly understood me. They're gone.

***

Awake again. I didn't want to wake up. I wanted to stay asleep forever. I don't want to be here. I want to be with them. I don't want to be in this hospital bed, I want to be dead.

Everyone is in my room. The Devis. Both sets of Diazes. My parents. Nurses, doctors. They're all staring at me, processing the fact that I'm the only one alive.

I somehow am always thinking about that fact and refusing to think about it at the same time. I don't want to think about it. I don't want to believe it.

189

If it's true, I'm alone. If I'm alone, I'm back where I was three years ago. If I'm back there, I've made no progress. If I've made no progress, I'm still suicidal. I'm still a scared little kid who wishes to be gone.

I don't know what to do. I don't know anything. I need routine, but I've been thrown off mine entirely. I need safety, but there is nothing safe about what's going on. I don't know what to do.

"I don't like this," I whisper, my voice getting caught in the back of my throat. My mom leaps up from her chair and pulls me into a hug.

Roxanne is like my sister. I have very few childhood memories that don't include her. Our lives have been intertwined since the day I left the womb. I have never known a life without her. She shows me that life isn't always hurt, it can be beautiful. She's incredible. She was incredible.

Jessie understands me in a way no one else ever has. We have a secret language that only we can speak. They are the kindest, most generous person I have ever met. I hate the fact that they've felt some of the same awful things I have. They're so kind. They were so kind.

Otto was always the friend I wished I had. I spent years imagining what our friendship would be like. The real thing is so much better. We don't need to speak. A single glance or head nod and we'll bust a gut laughing. We understand the same jokes, we want the same things. I never feel weird when I'm around him. He can always make me smile. He could always make me smile.

It shouldn't have been like this. I was the driver, shouldn't I have died? I added the least to the group. I'm not kind, I'm not cool, I'm not funny. It should have been me. It should have been me with the aneurysm. It should have been me bleeding out on the side of the road. It shouldn't have been me sitting in this hospital bed. I shouldn't have survived. I deserve to have died.

I don't know if I can handle this. The first day of summer is in a week, but I'm not going to school until then. The doctors say I'll be able to go swimming by then. How the hell would I be able to go swimming? The most important people in the world aren't in the world anymore, and I am.

It's not fair.

Chapter Twenty-Five

It can't be true. This can't be happening. The last two months... how?

They tell me I passed out right on Jessie's front porch. I was taken back to my house and laid down on my bed. When I woke back up, my parents were in my room speaking in hushed voices. It reminds me of a time not that long ago, a time I forgot. A hospital bed, pain, hushed voices coming from worried parents.

They asked if I thought they were still alive. I don't understand. I hung out with them yesterday, but they told me they died on prom night. Prom night? I don't remember prom night, but I assumed it was because I got drunk or something.

Not this.

They're gone? They can't be gone. Who do I have if they're gone? What happened this summer? The bucket list... the wedding... tattoos? Did that actually happen?

My wrist is still sore. There is still a sunset inked into it. I refuse to believe that I'm the only one with this tattoo. I refuse to believe that their wrists are bare and six feet underground. That can't be true.

I've been all alone all summer? All summer... everything I've done, I've been doing by myself? I went cliff jumping by myself, I got a tattoo by myself, I egged Gail's house by myself?

I need proof. There's no way. This is all some sick prank. Some way to freak me out. Everyone has seen them this summer. Muriel, the woman at the tattoo parlor. They have to be able to tell me they're still here. They can't be gone. It doesn't make any sense.

"I don't believe you," I tell my parents when they're done explaining. Memories tug at my brain, begging to be released, and acknowledged, but I can't. I can't remember, because that makes them gone. They can't be gone.

I fling myself out of bed and all the way to my car. I don't play music, even though I always do. I don't play music today.

My parents are standing on my porch, crying out for me to stop. I can't talk to them. I pull out of the parking lot and drive down the street. To Otto's house. His dad's car isn't there. Why isn't it there? His brother is still in the window. Why is he in the window?

I can't go to Jessie's house again, that's where it got ruined. That's where the lies started. They have to be lies.

I can't go to Roxanne's again. Mrs. Devi has probably been talking to my parents. I can't deal with that. They're all wrong, everyone is wrong. They are alive, they're somewhere. They're hiding.

I can't go back to my house, so I pull out onto the highway. Cars whiz past me, no idea that I'm currently in the middle of a mental crisis.

If I crash my car now, it'll all be over. I won't have to think about if it is true. I don't have to think about the fact that I'm alone. It's not a fact, it's a possibility.

I end up back at the tattoo parlor. I don't know what to do. I guess I should go inside, and see if the girl remembers them.

She's sweeping the floor inside, her chair empty.

"Hello?" I whisper. She turns to look at me.

"Hey. Are you here for another one? I'm free." She grins.

"No, I wanted to talk about the last time I was here. I was with my friends, right? They were tattooed by some people in the back?"

"Um. I was the only one working that day. I'm not sure what you mean by 'people in the back'. That's just the break room." She gestures to the curtain and then places her hand on her phone. She thinks I'm insane. She thinks she might need to call the cops. Some crazy girl is seeing things. She's seeing dead people, ghosts.

I'm crazy.

I ran out of the store faster than a bullet. This can't be right. Any second now, I'm going to wake up. I'm going to wake up to a bunch of texts from my friends, asking me to hang out.

The texts. That's got to be proof that they were actually there.

In the parked car, I pick up and scroll through my text messages. But... they're gone. I thought they texted me last night. Something about a funeral...?

Oh.

Oh fuck.

No. This is–

All my friends are gone. I'm never going to see them again. I'm never going to see my favorite people ever again.

What about our plans? Last summer before university, last summer together. Last summer before they died.

This isn't supposed to happen like this.

I want to pull my car out of its spot. I want to drive, drive far away, and maybe crash my car on the way. But I can't move. I'm stuck. My hands are frozen on the last texts. Texts from Roxanne to the group on the way to prom.

'We're coming to pick you up. You ready?'

I want to scream no. I want to yell at us to not leave, to ditch prom, stay home, and watch movies. Anything. I wish with every fiber of my soul that we got the flu and couldn't go. I wish with every drop of my blood that the car didn't start. No amount of wishing makes it disappear — No amount of wishing makes the truth disappear.

I can't breathe. I can't breathe. I'm dying.

Dying.

I wish. I wish I was dying of natural causes right now so I wouldn't have to keep fighting. So it wouldn't be as shameful as suicide. So people wouldn't blame it on me or my parents.

I just want to be gone.

***

When I was in ninth grade, I wanted more than anything to go to a mental hospital. I wanted to have a failed suicide attempt so they would make me stay in the hospital until I felt better.

They might send me to the psychiatric ward now. Seeing people isn't something that people usually do. Feeling people... hearing them... believing they truly exist. People who have died.

That isn't something people usually do.

I regret wanting to go there in grade nine. I don't want to go there anymore. I don't want them to be gone. I want them to come back. I want to stay sick so they come back.

"Come back!" I scream, still in a parked car outside of a tattoo parlor. At this point, I don't even care if anyone hears me.

"Come back!" My voice crumples into sobs. Why aren't they back? Why are they still gone? They were here once, can't they do it again? I need to see them again. I can't be alone again. I need them to come back.

A pedestrian knocks on my window, wondering if I'm okay. I flash the fakest smile soaked in tears, letting him know he can go away. He does. I don't need some random stranger to make me feel okay. I need them back to be okay. I need to talk to my people. *My people.*

"Come back. I can't do this without you."

Chapter Twenty-Six

I haven't left my bed for days. I've been either watching movies or crying. I haven't slept, I haven't eaten.

I have to get out of bed today. It's the funeral. They delayed it for a while — one and a half months to be exact — because everyone was so in shock. They wanted to make sure I could go. I have to go.

Before I do anything, I need to have a shower. I also need to change my bedsheets at some point today. They're stained and smelly. I don't want to do any of that, but if I'm getting out of bed, I might as well.

I don't use any nice-smelling soap or anything in the shower. I don't deserve that today. I end up using my dad's shampoo, just so I smell the least happy as possible. It's kind of ridiculous, but I don't know what to do for funerals. I've never been to one before.

I do know that you have to wear black to funerals. Formal black attire. I don't have any formal black attire. I have a green dress from a Christmas party last year and the cheesy powder blue dress that Otto and I bought for the wedding. Along with the black dress that Roxanne wore. I suppose it is black, but it wouldn't fit me. And I could never wear her wedding dress to her funeral.

That's when it hits me.

The wedding. Didn't actually happen. I went to a thrift store, bought four outfits, and acted out a wedding by myself.

Crazy.

I also have my prom dress. Prom.

It's buried at the back of my closet. I haven't looked at it in months. I need to look at it.

I don't remember putting it back there, but I know it is there.

It is there. The floral embroidery pattern is stained rust red. There are rips across the skirt and one of the sleeves is nearly detached. Oh god, is that my blood or theirs? Is that the last piece of them I have? Dried blood on a once beautiful, now shitty, prom dress.

I hate to think about how happy I was when I first saw this dress. I hate to think about how confident I was. I hate to think about any time when I wasn't as miserable as I am right now.

I deserve to be dead.

Misery is what I deserve. I hate thinking about how naive I was before I realized that life sucks. Before, when my biggest problem was wanting to kill myself.

I had no reason to want that. Now I do. Now I have a reason. No one would blame me. I could take that fucking dress and wrap it around my neck, choking myself. I could turn it into a fucking noose.

No. I can't. If I showed up in the afterlife, they would never forgive me.

The afterlife doesn't exist. They're gone forever.

It might. I have to think that it might exist. I have to think that they are watching me, making jokes and bets about what I'll do. I have to believe that Jessie and Roxanne are living together, happy and alone finally. I have to believe that Otto is finally okay. That he'll be okay.

He's dead.

He's dead, it doesn't fucking matter if he's okay. He's not here anymore. He's gone. He's not frolicking in the afterlife. He's been chewed up by bugs and fungus underground.

My mom walks in. She stares at me staring at the dress.

"Cecelia? Are you okay?" She places a hand on my shoulder.

"I... don't know what to wear," I say, voice quivering. I can't cry again. It's pointless to cry.

I cry anyway.

"It's okay honey. I have an extra dress you can wear."

She leaves and returns with the most ridiculous-looking dress. I think it might genuinely be a smock. Yet, it's the right thing to wear.

Roxanne would've cried if she saw me wearing this. She would've instantly made me go shopping for a hot funeral outfit. She'll never do that though, because she's gone.

I don't like this.

Dad, Mom, and I walk the three blocks to the church. There's a joint funeral for them there. They would've hated this. A church? Again, Roxanne would've cried. Otto would've shrugged and Jessie would've sighed.

This should have been at the lake. Or in my basement. Somewhere they love — loved. Somewhere that actually has a bit of them in it. This isn't right at all.

I want to go home.

I pull on my mom's sleeve like a little kid, begging to go home. She shakes her head, her eyes watering.

"We have to go to this, Cecelia, I'm sorry. They need you there."

"Who? My friends? They don't need me, they need heartbeats and working lungs. I don't think they care very much."

"Not them. Their families. They're counting on you to be there."

When we enter the church, I see that it's true. Mrs. Devi's face lights up, just slightly. Her eyes glisten, whether with tears or gratefulness, possibly both. Across the room, she mouths words at me. "Thank you."

I don't know why she cares if I'm here. I don't know what that means to anyone. I'm a mess who doesn't deserve to mourn their children. I'm a mess who killed them.

Had they never befriended me, they would still be alive. Had I never randomly spoken to Otto walking home from a hockey game, he would still be alive. Had I never let them come into Ms. Wilson's room during lunch, they would still be alive.

Had I listened to the anxiety/depression/whatever on prom night, I wouldn't be here. Someone else would have driven, someone else would have seen the car earlier. Someone else would have swerved away from it.

Whenever Jessie was spiraling like this, I'd tell them that they couldn't change the past. I'd tell them that passed is passed. I can't tell myself that. I'm still stuck there, replaying every single variation of every single action. Watching as I die, watching as they live. Life, death, record scratch. Happy, sad, record scratch.

A piano starts playing classic American funeral songs. It's not how it's supposed to be. Otto once told me to make sure they play heavy metal at his funeral to lighten the vibe. This isn't right at all. I guess it's too late to change it now.

Jessie's mom makes her way onto the stage, her shaking hands grasping lined yellow paper. She goes on to speak about how incredible they were. How kind, how sweet. How when they were five, they picked up an old lady's sweater when she dropped it.

The speech is all wrong. She keeps misgendering them. Why? They came out to her. I know she hates it, but it's their funeral, shouldn't she be respectful?

It hits me like a ton of bricks. How do I keep forgetting these things? Jessie wasn't alive when they came out to her. They were already dead. That never fucking happened. I laid on Jessie's lawn by myself for an hour before pretending like everything went well.

That's not actually how the Diazes reacted. They haven't reacted yet. They don't even know. They will never know one of the biggest parts of their own child's life. I'm the only person on the planet that will remember to address them correctly.

They'll be something they're not forever.

I relate to that statement. I'll never be myself again. How could I? When the only people that know the true me are gone?

Chapter Twenty-Seven

Twelfth Grade, May

We're starting to get scared. What if we're not friends when we go to university? What if we lose everything we've built over the past three years?

Jessie made a plan. We'll trade things that we'll keep in our dorm rooms so we'll always remember each other. Something that reminds us of each other, something special.

We're exchanging our gifts tonight during our weekly sleepover. I'm a little nervous; what if my gifts aren't good enough? What if everyone else's are incredible and mine suck? I couldn't deal with that.

The gifts suck. Everyone hates you.

God. I'm so done with those thoughts. I'm so done with self-loathing. I wish I could make it go away, and become one of those girls on the internet who are constantly happy and confident. I know, I know. Social media isn't real life. But they love themselves so much. How is that possible? Even right now, as I'm thinking about this, I'm staring into the mirror, hating the way my face looks, the way my neck looks.

I pull out my phone to watch videos with confidence tips. I have a whole collection saved. Millions of worthless tips. Wear your cutest outfit, and say affirmations. I could never.

I am confident.

No, you're not.

I am beautiful.

Why would you say that? What kind of self-obsessed narcissist are you?

It just doesn't work for me.

The doorbell rings downstairs. Damn, is it already five? It's only four forty. Who's here? Is it the police? An ax murderer?

Jessie's at the door, a cardboard shoebox in their arms.

"Hey!" I smile, acting like I wasn't just pointing out my every flaw. I am a chill happy person.

"Hi! I know I'm a little early, but I couldn't wait."

"Oh, are you? I didn't notice."

Ha ha.

Me, not noticing something terrifying. As if.

It's Jessie's turn to pick the movie today. They pick a tear-jerker romance movie we've seen fifty billion times.

"It's a classic summer movie!" they claim.

I guess.

Otto and Roxanne show up around the same time, Roxanne holding a tote bag and Otto with a backpack. They all have amazing gifts. Mine are probably nowhere as good.

They head downstairs, rolling their eyes when they see which movie Jessie has selected.

"Again?" Otto groans.

"Again!" Jessie grins.

"Okay, but we have to trade our things first, right?" Roxanne confirms. "I literally don't think I can wait any longer."

"Okay, chill, let's do it." Otto takes a seat on the floor and opens his backpack. "How are we doing this?"

"Um... you go first?" I suggest. I'm nervous. I don't want to go first, but I also don't want to go last. I want to go in the middle, so I have no impact whatsoever. That's the recipe for success.

Otto passes out wrapped packages. Mine is a large rectangle. It was stretching out the edges of his backpack.

Jessie starts to open their package, gasping when they see the contents. It's a... necklace?

"What's up with that?" I ask.

"Um yeah." Otto smiles. "I wasn't sure what to do for Jessie, since we'll obviously keep seeing each other after university at family reunions and stuff. This was our grandma's. Since she had two sons, she gave it to the older one, my dad. He had two sons, so I asked if I could give it to Jessie."

"Oh my god, Otto." Tears start to run down their cheeks. I look at Roxanne instead of them so they can have a nice cousin moment.

After wiping their face with their sleeve, they gesture at Roxanne. "Open yours next," they instruct.

She tears open the paper and bursts out laughing when she pulls out her present. All I can see is that it's a black crewneck sweater.

"I know we weren't technically supposed to buy anything, but I saw this and thought it was just too perfect for her," Otto explains.

"What does it say?" I demand.

Roxanne flips it around so we can see the bubble letters pasted on the front. 'I heart ur mom.'

"Oh wow, that is beautiful." I chuckle as she pulls it over her head.

"Okay, Cecelia, it's your turn!" she insists.

I flip my rectangle over, slitting the tape with a fingernail. I attempt to remove the paper without damaging it, but everyone starts yelling at me to tear it up, so I just rip it. From the back, it looks like a canvas or something. When I turn it to the front, I instantly let out a gasp.

"Otto," I murmur. "This is beautiful. Holy shit."

It's a watercolor painting of four flowers. A red poppy, a yellow rose, a sprig of lavender, and a deep blue periwinkle. They feel vaguely familiar.

"Is it—" I start, unaware of how to finish.

"It's us." He grins.

"What is it?!" Roxanne yells, scooching over so she can see. "Am I the poppy?" she asks.

"Yeah."

"Whoa."

"Thank you, dude," I choke. "This is perfect." I don't want to stop hanging out with these guys next year. I want to be friends until the day we die.

"Okay someone else go," Otto says, waving his hand at us.

Roxanne opens her tote bag and passes us all items. "I didn't know that we were supposed to wrap them, so they were all just chilling in my bag. She hands me a t-shirt, one that I recognize instantly.

"Roxanne," I sigh. "I can't take this."

"Yeah, you can. I'm not that attached to it, but you love it. You've been taking it since junior high."

Not that attached to it? It's her favorite shirt. The brown one with the map of Manhattan. The one I steal basically every day.

I wrap her in a hug. I can't believe she gave this to me. I can't believe we were barely friends for a couple of years. She's my sister.

"Okay, my turn, my turn!" Jessie announces. This means I'm going to have to go last. I guess I can live with that.

Jessie passes out an array of items, starting with Roxanne. It's a ring.

"Oh, damn, are you proposing?" I ask.

"No." They laugh. "It's a promise ring. You don't have to wear it if you don't want to, I just—"

"I'm going to wear it." Roxanne slides it onto her ring finger, the one you put wedding rings on. This seems an awful lot like a proposal.

211

Jessie pulls Floppy out of the box and passes him to me.

"Floppy?" I look the tattered brown bunny in the eyes, smiling at the familiarity.

"Yeah. For when you're in university and you make all these cool friends that like horror movies. You need him more than I do."

"Bold of you to assume I'll make friends."

"You will," they assure me. "I know you don't believe me, but you will."

Maybe I'll make friends. Maybe I'll find people in one of my classes. Maybe I'll join a book club. Maybe I'll meet people that understand me, all the parts of me. Maybe I'll befriend people that love me for who I am and will never judge me.

Maybe I'll make friends. But no one on earth will be as incredible and perfect as the friends I have in Lake Oublie.

Chapter Twenty-Eight

Today I'm moving into the dorms. It's the inevitable moment. The moment I've been waiting for since eighth grade. I read this thing once that says you can't heal in the same place you got sick.

I suppose I got sick in Lake Oublie. Today, I'm leaving so I can finally heal. Today, I'm going to get better.

It's been two months since they died. It's been a month since I realized. It's getting better. Slowly, but ever so slightly, It's getting better. I haven't cried in a while. A couple of days, at least.

It's hard to leave. It's hard to step out of the house for the last time. It's hard to realize that I'm leaving the last place I saw my friends. The only place I've ever lived. Where I took my first steps, spoke my first words, cried my first tears.

Made my first friends.

I don't think I'm ready to leave, but it doesn't matter. It's time. It's time to start the next part of my life, the adult part. The on-my-own part.

I expected to feel different today. I expected to cry as I left my house. I expected to want to listen to nostalgic songs in the car. I expected to feel something.

I just want to go back. Not to my house, but to my childhood. To the years before I knew what intrusive thoughts meant. Before I ever heard the name Otto Diaz. I want to relive my time with them. I would have cherished it so much more had I known it would be so limited.

It's okay. I can't keep replaying it. I need to move on. Not forget they existed, not forget what they meant to me. To remember without the pain. To be able to live again. To want to live again.

Looking out the airplane window onto the approaching buildings in Montreal, I do want to live again.

You shouldn't.

I want to go swimming again. I want to laugh again. I want to publish one of my stories. I want to save a life like they saved mine. I want to grow up, I want to get a house on my own and decorate it how I like. This is my first step. Right now is my first step.

Leaving the airport. Cab ride. Head out the window, buildings whizzing past.

I can't believe I'm going to live in this city for the next four years of my life, at least.

I snap a picture of the red leaves on a maple tree and send it to the group chat. Old habits die hard.

I wish I was getting photos of their cities, and their universities. It's okay that I'm not. It'll be okay that I'm not.

I'm already in love with Montreal. I picked the right city. There are so many people walking dogs on the sidewalk. Snippets of conversations in French drift into the taxi. They're speaking so quickly that I can barely understand. Thirteen years of French immersion is still not enough.

I'm so excited. I haven't been this excited in a really, really, long time.

The campus is beautiful. The students look like everything I've ever wanted to be. Smiling, chatting, laughing. Soon, that'll be me.

The parking lot is filled to the brim with soon-to-be freshmen and their parents. It's possible someone here will be my closest friend in a year. That's insane.

I try to smile at as many people as I can muster, wincing when they look me up and down. If I had to take a guess, they probably won't be my closest friends.

Dorky-looking students are standing all over the campus handing out pamphlets and maps. My mom runs up to them and starts to ask them thousands of questions.

I'm utterly humiliated, but at the same time, I really want to know the answers to all of her questions.

At least she's not the only one. Nearly every single guide is swarmed with overprotective parents. There's a family a couple of feet from us in the exact same position. The daughter, a girl with rosy cheeks and fiery red hair smiles at me, laughing at our parents. I roll my eyes in their direction. She snickers.

I want to talk to her, but the guide gives us instructions on where we should go to find my room, so we have to leave.

My room is on the seventh floor, which is awesome. Seven is my favorite number. It's a good sign.

My roommate isn't here yet. I get the first pick of a bed, I guess. I choose the one closest to the door. I know that's an unpopular opinion, murderers or whatever, but I like it better. Easier to make a quick escape if necessary.

My parents help me unpack all the giant, important stuff, but when it comes to the more personal stuff, they stop.

"We'll go set up a mailbox for you," my mom says.

"Do I even need a mailbox? Isn't most stuff digital now?"

"Nope, bank statements are still sent by mail." My dad opens the door for my mom and closes it behind him.

I take as long as possible putting away all my clothes and books, but it's eventually time to face the inevitable.

I have one small tote bag at the bottom of all my stuff. It's filled with things I haven't been able to look at in months, things that I've got just for today.

The first thing I take out is Floppy. The ratty brown rabbit that'll keep nightmares away.

Jessie.

Floppy goes on my bed, tucked under the covers. Although it's ridiculous, I kiss him on the forehead.

The next item is the shirt. The beautiful vintage map of New York on the coffee-coloured background.

Roxanne.

I press it into my nose and inhale, taking in her faded smell. Cinnamon and cherry pie. I miss that smell. I miss how strong it was in her house, in her room.

I pull off my tank top and replace it with the shirt. The cotton is soft against my skin from years of use.

I prepare myself to look at the last item. The one that I've been dreading looking at since I arrived. I have the perfect spot for it, a blank wall right above my bed.

I dig my hand down to the very bottom of the bag and wrap my fingers around the corner of the canvas.

Otto.

I forgot how beautiful this painting is. I forgot how he perfectly captured our essences with flowers. I forgot how talented he was.

She's so quiet, I barely hear her come in, but I hear her speak.

"That's gorgeous."

I forgot that I'd have a roommate. I forgot someone else will see this every day.

I turn around to see the red-haired girl. She's got her hands full of suitcases, so I go to help her.

"Hi," I greet. "I'm Cecelia."

"Nelly." She shakes my hand. "Well, my name is Cornelia, actually, but Nelly's what everyone calls me. Did you paint that?" She gestures towards the painting.

I stare at it, pain hollow in my chest. But there's a feeling stronger than pain now. Pride.

"I didn't," I say, a smile on my face. "My best friend did."

Acknowledgements

Oh my god, where do I even start with these? Bear with me, I'm going to list a lot of people here.

First of all, thank you to my editor, Cheyenne Nielsen. I can't believe how lucky I was that you reached out to me. That you wanted to edit my book. I couldn't ask for a better editor, thank you, thank you, thank you.

Thank you to all of my beta readers, Ellie, Palak, Alina, Millie, Yfke, and Remus. You guys are hilarious and it was so much fun to see you react to the story.

Thank you to all of my alpha readers, my mom (who takes that job very seriously), Olivia, Aviva, Auntie Jen, Audrey, and Lizzy. (I'll talk more about y'all more in detail later don't worry.)

To everyone at work who randomly answered all of my strange questions about books. Madeline, who wholly supported me and was so kind and incredible. Olivia, Kiera, and Miles, who just accepted my weird questions about how big a book should be and if I should make the pages white or yellow.

To Georgia Montgomery, who created the most incredible cover for this book, thank you for just jumping on board and making my crazy scribbled idea real.

Thank you to Kathleen and Shauneen, the therapist and counselor that kept me (somewhat) sane during the creation of this story.

I'm so grateful to everyone on Instagram, I would list you guys but there are so many names I can't. Everyone who dm-ed me with excitement for my book, asked questions, anything and everything.

To Millie, Yfke, and Tokyoyume, whose books I beta read. It kept me excited to keep writing and also you guys are incredible omg.

Thank you to my family, to my grandpa for expanding my vocabulary, Annie Grandma for also being a writer, Grandma for all her excitement about this even before she knew anything about the plot, and Auntie Jen (I know you're not technically my family but you're awesome). To my parents for all of the love and support you've shown me, thank you for everything. To Shea, you're pretty cool I guess. Also, thanks for setting up the open mic and listening to *Karma (Featuring Ice Spice)* with me afterward.

Thank you to any of my friends that showed remotely any interest in my book. Georgia, Ella, Peyton, Dasha, Angelina, Cedar, Ava, I hope I'm not forgetting anyone.

To Lizzy, the co-writer of Project Broken, who made edits of this book and kept me excited about it the entire time. Thank you for listening to songs 'from Otto's perspective', for helping me plot, and for sending me pictures of you crying while reading.

To Audrey, I don't even know how to thank you enough for this. You were just there for me the entire time, you listened to me describe the plot forty thousand times; you were just perfect and incredible thank you thank you thank you.

Finally, thank you to anyone who picked this book up and read it. To anyone who actually spent money on it (what???) and read it. I am infinitely grateful to you. You are the coolest people ever, I am your number one fan.

13139183R00129